AUG 1 2 2015

W9-BGJ-034

The Nonprofit
Survival Guide

NAPA COUNTY LIBRARY
580 COOMBS STREET
NAPA, CA 94559

AUG 3 1 2015

ALSO BY GEOFF ALEXANDER

---

*Films You Saw in School: A Critical Review
of 1,153 Classroom Educational Films (1958–1985)
in 74 Subject Categories* (McFarland, 2014)

Academic Films for the Classroom: A History
(McFarland, 2010)

The Nonprofit Survival Guide

A Strategy for Sustainability

GEOFF ALEXANDER

McFarland & Company, Inc., Publishers
Jefferson, North Carolina

LIBRARY OF CONGRESS CATALOGUING-IN-PUBLICATION DATA

Alexander, Geoff, 1952–
    The nonprofit survival guide : a strategy for sustainability /
Geoff Alexander.
        p.   cm.
    Includes bibliographical references and index.

    ISBN 978-0-7864-9844-4 (softcover : acid free paper) ∞
    ISBN 978-1-4766-2050-3 (ebook)

    1. Nonprofit organizations—Management.   2. Nonprofit
organizations.   I. Title.
    HD62.6.A435 2015
    658'.048—dc23   2015017730

BRITISH LIBRARY CATALOGUING DATA ARE AVAILABLE

© 2015 Geoff Alexander. All rights reserved

No part of this book may be reproduced or transmitted in any form
or by any means, electronic or mechanical, including photocopying
or recording, or by any information storage and retrieval system,
without permission in writing from the publisher.

Front cover image © 2015 iStock/Thinkstock

Printed in the United States of America

McFarland & Company, Inc., Publishers
  Box 611, Jefferson, North Carolina 28640
    www.mcfarlandpub.com

Acknowledgments

The genesis for this book was sparked by a common remark people would make while discussing what we were accomplishing here at the Academic Film Archive of North America with limited funding: "I just don't know how you folks do it." Everyone can do it, I thought, but you've got to start with exceptional core volunteers such as the ones we have. In one way or another, they're part of many of the examples and anecdotes included in this book. So thank you, Scott and Debbie Edmonson, Dan and Karen Greenbank, Jerome Mallory, Rob and Kirsten McGlynn, Margie Newman, Barinda Samra, Michael Selic, and Bruce Wakayama.

Writers tend to be their own worst proofreaders, and I'd guess that every writer still finds nitpicky errors in his or her published books that all the proofreading in the world didn't seem to catch. Proofreading a manuscript is an arduous task, so special thanks go out to Carson "Kit" Davidson, Jim Reed, and Audrey Wong for reading this one and catching errors and omissions along the way. Jim and Audrey also read the manuscript for content and made it a point to question and occasionally criticize what they were reading. We didn't always agree, and the book is stronger because of it. I received much help for the case studies as well, so thank you to Rick Holden and Sandy Moll, Helen and Rod MacKinlay, Bente Torjusen of AVA Gallery, David Fairbanks Ford of the Main Street Museum, and especially Craig Diserens of Village Harvest, Jenny Do of Friends of Hue, and Roxanne Valladao of Plumas Arts.

The greatest thanks of all, though, goes to that large and important world of nonprofit volunteers. You might be one of them. You put in way too much time, don't get thanked enough, imperil your family and

Acknowledgments

social life, and sometimes get called "crazy" for your passion to make your world—and ours—a better place. Your nobility, cheerfulness in the face of challenges, and work ethic continue to inspire us all, in and out of the nonprofit world, to greater heights. Writers often dedicate their books to individuals who inspire them, but I want to tell you, I thought about all you volunteers as I wrote every page of this book. You continue to make it all worthwhile.

Table of Contents

Table of Contents

Preface

What is a guerrilla nonprofit? As the founder of a small but successful one, I did not at first realize our organization was a guerrilla group. Then I began writing this book. Some of the techniques we used to start with (not having paid employees, not paying rent, not having a substantial number of board members, and not applying for large grants, for example) were just that—techniques that we used successfully. At this point I began perusing the literature on building nonprofits. And I realized that many of our ideas might be considered radical ones. Many of them flew in the face of recommendations I encountered in just about every book I read. At first, I thought that some of our different approaches might very well work for heavily funded organizations but would be no use to small ones. But it soon became apparent that these ideas were in fact even more critical for smaller nonprofits than for the bigger ones. Large or small, all such organizations can become successful and sustainable by using the techniques associated with what I've come to call "the guerrilla nonprofit."

I'm not big on war metaphors. They're often overused and imprecise. *Merriam-Webster's Collegiate Dictionary* (which calls itself "The Voice of Authority"), though, defines the term "guerrilla" as a noun, in part, as "a person who engages in irregular warfare especially as a member of an independent unit," and as an adjective, "of, relating to, or characteristic of guerrillas esp. in being aggressive, radical, or unconventional."[1] This book is a guide for an "independent unit" wishing to build or evolve a nonprofit, tax-exempt corporation by being aggressively savvy, opportunistic, and unconventional.

There is precedence for this notion. In my first book, *Academic Films for the Classroom: A History*, I describe how the United States government, through edicts such as the Elementary and Secondary Educational Act, facilitated the funneling of money to companies making educational films. The funds were given to educational entities such as school districts, which then used them to buy films. As I suggested, it was essentially a socialist venture embedded in a framework of capitalism. And it's really not so different in the nonprofit world. Here public service is paid for by the public via grants, sponsorships, and donations. The government makes this tax deductible. Private capital, generally in the form of foundation grants, supports public benefit corporations as well. As you'll read further on, in addition to our main focus, that of providing a public service, our small nonprofit creates a side benefit that helps a few for-profit companies make money. The case studies in Appendix I prove that others do, too. Such nonprofit/for-profit partnerships have worked well for us. So we like it when our for-profit affiliates do well, too.

At first glance, large, well-funded nonprofits may feel they won't derive much from this book. After all, they have large boards and sometimes a plethora of paid employees, funded by successful applications made to large granting agencies. If you are an officer, employee, or volunteer for a larger nonprofit, I encourage you, however, to think again and reconsider where you are in terms of efficiency and sustainability. Losing out on a big grant can force even large nonprofits to consider new ways to trim unneeded costs and do better with less. We are now in a time when there are more nonprofits than ever, trying to take more slices out of a diminishing number of pies.

Just how many nonprofits are there, anyway? In the introduction I will provide some statistics, but here are a few for starters. In 2008 (the last year when such statistics were available), there were 974,337 501(c)(3) public charities in the United States. Roughly half of them either were not making as much as $25,000 per year or simply didn't bother filing a tax return. Further, statistics indicated that approximately 727 new nonprofits were being formed each week, based on a ten-year average. That's a huge number of nonprofits competing for funding.

Much of what the pundits are prescribing for existing nonprofits— particularly smaller ones—just isn't working. These organizations have the drive, but often they perceive that they just don't have enough resources. As I'll point out here, they actually do have the resources, but they need to change their approach to utilizing them—aggressively and, on many occasions, unconventionally. And individuals in the process of starting a nonprofit, or just thinking about it, need to restart, rethink, and possibly even reimagine. If you're in the stage of considering whether to form a nonprofit, though, do understand that it will take hard work and a lot of time. The rewards, however, are significant, in terms of public service and the personal satisfaction you'll derive from helping to make your world a better place. Small, creative, cutting-edge, and sustainable nonprofits are the wave of the future. They can and do serve the public well and successfully.

This book is here to tell you how, and I encourage you to take notes, right in the text. A good way is to keep a pencil handy, bracket what you like on a page, then write those page numbers with a couple of key words on the blank pages at the end. When you've finished, you can then review the notes you took and compile them for a list of your own action items. Every nonprofit, or soon-to-be nonprofit, is different. Your notes will vary depending on if you're a start-up or mature organization. But I guarantee you, you will find much in this book to be compelling reading, regardless of your situation. In our constantly changing world, the creation of new ideas is critical to the success of every nonprofit, and I'm willing to bet that the discussions in this book will compel you to engender your own.

Introduction:
I'm Small ... Why
Should I Bother Forming
a Nonprofit Corporation?

You've got the Grand Vision. You're a subject matter expert, have a passion for what you do and love. It's gone way beyond being a hobby that took up a few hours in your spare time. It's now become a real vocation in itself and it's taking up most of your waking and weekend hours. Your friends and family are involved, and you now want to share it with the world in the biggest way you can. You've put much time and hard work into building your dream, and you've cobbled together those acquaintances who are working with you to perform important tasks and publicize what you're doing and how you're doing it. You've pretty much funded everything yourself up until now, but you've recognized that you can't do that forever. You've determined that seeking charitable contributions may be a way to allow your passion to remain viable for years to come. In addition, you've realized that having a charitable nonprofit organization could provide you with the cachet you'd like for forming relationships with scholars, experts, and selected nonprofits that have aims and audiences similar to yours.

You are not alone. Consider again the statistics I introduced in the Preface. As recently as 2008—the last calendar year from which the IRS derived decade-specific statistics—the number of 501(c)(3) public charities in the United States totaled 974,337. More than half of these (490,558) were listed by the IRS as being either Non-Reporting or reporting less than $25,000 in annual Gross Receipts. These figures had grown significantly from a decade earlier, a 1998 total of 596,169, with a combined Non-Reporting and under $25,000 Gross Receipts number of 364,535.[1] In ten years, the total of such charities therefore grew by 378,168. That's a staggering 727 per week over that ten-year period. The trend indicates that two things are happening. More and more of these public charities are forming all the time, while a vast number, approximately half a million of them, are struggling financially to survive.

Some people manage to do it all on their own as individual enterprises and never form a 501(c)(3) tax-exempt charitable corporation. Carson "Kit" Davidson, a noted filmmaker (http://archive.org/details/ThirdAve1950) who had a vision of building a hiking preserve in the mountains of Vermont, bought 420 acres at $69 an acre a number of years ago to build it. It's thriving, and he did it all without forming a nonprofit (http://www.afana.org/taconic.htm). You can do that, too. But countless others, wanting to engage more people and funding, have formed small nonprofit charitable organizations. And that's why we're here now. This is not a "how to" legal book—although it does discuss some fundamental legal issues—but rather a road map to nonprofit sustainability. It illustrates how to accomplish your mission realistically on a relatively small amount of money and be able to thrive when financial times are tight. It's about avoiding pitfalls, too. I provide a number of examples based on the nonprofit organization of which I'm the director, but other nonprofit directors and managers have added their own suggestions as well. We've all had our successes and made our mistakes in the process. This book will help you to replicate the former while avoiding the latter.

There are a number of books on the market geared toward people running nonprofit organizations who are actively engaged in seeking ways to get millions of dollars in funding. These larger groups are engaged in mass-market fund raising efforts that might include direct mail and telemarketing and they often spend great amounts of time writing grant applications. Often, they are social purpose organizations, engaged in efforts such as feeding starving children, housing the homeless, and curing cancer. They have gathered millions of dollars in grant funds and probably have someone called a Development Director or some such title. This book will be of value to them, as guerrilla strategies and tactics are extremely useful, as the reality of numerous other large nonprofits eating away at diminishing grant sources causes these organizations to rethink the way they do business and subsequently to downsize their operations.

On the other hand, there are wonderful, insightful people with amazing passions for things and causes that don't resonate with most large funding organizations. They are stellar in their clarity of vision, purpose, and drive and are usually engaged in ensuring that the objects of their passions don't remain obscure and ignored by history. Eventually, they turn their passions into nonprofit organizations that may very well struggle with funding, due to the very obscurity of the subject that drove their passions. They certainly don't have a Development Officer, can't afford nonprofit consultants or mass mailings, and abhor making (or paying others to make) telemarketing calls. They probably don't have any employees. Still, they want a successful operation that may be underfunded but is sustainable. Sound familiar? Then read on.

You might have a passion for something unusual. It started as an interest, then became a hobby, and has now evolved into an all-encompassing cause. Could it be the *Rafflesia arnoldii*? That's a member of the genus *Rafflesia*, endemic to Borneo and Sumatra and famous for producing the largest individual flower on earth (it has a strong odor of decaying flesh, so it's often referred to as the "corpse flower"). Or perhaps you center your interests on the *ichigenkin*, a one-string Japanese zither that produces some of the starkest music on the planet. Or maybe your collection of glass telephone pole insulators has taken over your garage, your laundry room, your bedroom, and has caused your marriage to deteriorate. Your relationship will come to a crashing halt if you don't take the plunge and push your passion to the next step. So you're going to start a nonprofit organization. Once you get it launched, how do you make it successful and self-sustaining?

I refer to the proposed examples of Rafflesia, the ichigenkin, and insulators throughout the book, because people have passions for all manner of things, but groups and institutions that fund nonprofits working with more familiar areas of interest may very well not fund yours. Botany, music, and technology history aren't necessarily about saving the world. You may not be feeding starving children, finding a cure for cancer, housing the homeless, or creating an art and cultural experience that millions will enjoy, but will still require a brand-new building and a bunch of employees to operate. You're off on your own or with a few friends and fellow appreciators, enjoying your collection and passion. But turning your enthusiasm and drive into a valid non-profit organization does have its benefits.

For one, it gives you an imprimatur as an expert of sorts. It turns you from a hobbyist into an archivist or back-porch scholar. Armed with a great logo and an equally great website, you will attract people who share your passion or are only mildly interested but want to know more. You get to cajole, pontificate, instruct, and be a resource for thousands, maybe millions. Best of all, you get to infuse your passion into others.

You may, however, because of the esoteric nature of your passion, have trouble getting funded through grants. Yes, you will try, but like many budding book authors, you will collect enough rejection slips to pave your driveway. Your passion will not wither, but your desire to keep writing grant applications and requests for donations may soon fade. You will have to seek ways of funding that will go beyond writing grant applications and you'll have to be creative. You will need to adopt a "can-do" attitude, and laugh along with the occasional failures. For not every one of your efforts will work, even though you seemed to do everything right. You'll find, as I certainly did, that what others characterize as failures you'll think of instead as learning opportunities. And you'll get better at it all.

Don't Be Scared

You can do it, and I encourage you to. Grants aren't everything, but the time investment needed to apply for them and the fear of failure have frightened more than a few people away from even trying. Andrew Bales, president of Symphony Silicon Valley, not long ago said, "If you look around, nobody is creating a new arts organization anymore, and if they do, it's only with great trial and tribulation. The philanthropic environment with the recession now is simply about holding on to what you already have."[2] Bear in mind that Bales is headquartered in the high-tech capital of the country, where the regional economy is doing spectacularly in comparison with most others.

Introduction

There's real social value in making a success of a nonprofit that may not be all that grant-worthy, as long as you can make it sustainable. Many organizations that relied heavily on grants fell on hard times when the grant funding dried up, and a number of them folded. But yours won't, if you follow the threads in this book.

Although I focus on the nonprofit tax-exempt organizations that the Internal Revenue Service has designated as 501(c)(3)[3] public benefit corporations, much of what's here is applicable to organizations in the other Section 501 classes as defined by the IRS.[4] Sustainability, after all, is a universal construct.

I want to emphasize that others have been there before you. There's some work involved in starting a nonprofit and even more in making it operate successfully and sustainably. But believe me, it's gratifying and can be exhilarating, especially when you get your notification letter from the Internal Revenue Service. The IRS has created rules that work on your behalf, so learning how to work within them to accomplish your mission will make your organization stronger as it achieves its objectives. This applies to the paperwork that you'll fill out initially, as well as to decisions you'll make operationally when you receive your final notification that you're a valid nonprofit.

And perhaps most assuredly, please know that you are not alone, in this dark miasma of underfunded but culturally valuable nonprofits. I'll begin at the beginning, telling you what you'll need to get started. I'll give you some important and necessary resources you'll want to investigate as you begin forming your nonprofit, and provide a telescope into the future, in terms of what you can expect as you move your organization into the limelight. Also, how you'll survive when you hit the shadows as a cutting-edge, successful, and underfunded nonprofit.

That's right, I said cutting-edge. I also said successful. And underfunded. These might at first seem to be nonsequiturs. But here at the Academic Film Archive of North America, we've managed to make these words work together, for nearly fifteen years now. The words "successful" and "cutting-edge" aren't exactly objective, but as I'll describe later, you do have to define your own success. By our own definition, we're successful. We don't have a lot of money in the bank, but we're proud of how we've accomplished the goals of our mission and how we've continued to succeed. And you can, too. This book will show you how.

Here's an important item worth mentioning early on. For up-to-date information on tax laws regarding nonprofits, we always consult the IRS directly or seek the advice of a professional tax expert. I suggest you do the same. Laws are always evolving, so as a caveat, anything I discuss here, from a tax and general nonprofit law perspective, might have changed as the book went to press. There are a number of links to IRS web URLs in this book to help you, and Anthony Mancuso's excellent book *How to Form a Nonprofit Corporation,* discussed further in Chapter 3, "The First Step: Forming Your Nonprofit Organization," is highly recommended if you're just starting out.[5] The material included in this book is not to be considered as a substitute for legal counsel or professional tax advice but should enable your board officers, staff, and volunteers to carry on informed discussions with advisors in these areas of expertise.

What's in the Book?

Chapter 1 is a discussion of conceptualizing the term "success." In the nonprofit world, the success of your organization really depends on how you define it and how you'll then go about meeting the objectives addressed in your mission statement. The importance of keeping your day job is described in the second chapter, as sustainability requires that you seriously consider whether you'll initially want to have employees. Chapters 3 and 4 address some important milestones you'll encounter as you form your nonprofit. You'll have to keep some critical things in mind, particularly in terms of costs, as you set up your office

I'm a real believer in cost-effectively setting up and running a website that reflects the goals of your organization, as discussed in Chapter 5. Building an effective Keynote Program will be critical to receiving sponsorships and other means of funding and you'll need great volunteers to make it work, the topics addressed in chapters 6 and 7.

You'll want to consider staging events, attending conferences, and collecting important alliances and affiliates along the way. Chapters 8

Introduction

and 9 provide a road map to doing them efficiently and successfully. Thinking about publicity and publishing? You should and you'll find workable ideas on how to go about doing that in Chapter 10.

Chances are that you'll try the funding mill of grant applications and online funding platforms. The information in chapters 11 and 12 may help you avoid some pitfalls and keep it all in perspective. Chapter 13 provides more ideas on the value of thinking out of the box, trying new things, and being creative and sustainable in your approach to how you position your nonprofit.

Regardless of what you try, you really do want to operate on the good side of the law. It's deceptively easy, but you will need to keep a few important things in mind, as revealed in Chapter 14. In some ways, Chapter 15 is the most important one in the book. Throughout the life of your organization, you do have to document your assets and points of access, for your own benefit as well as for those who succeed you. Many small organizations don't think of this until it's too late, but it's a critical step in helping to ensure that your organization stays viable through emergencies. Chapter 16 discusses the value of staying small, manageable, and sustainable, which is where you'll begin and where you might actually want to stay.

Ready to begin? This book is loaded with points of discussion, items for thought, and plenty of "been there, done that" examples. Turn the page and let's get started.

CHAPTER 1

Redefining "Success"

I recognize that some discussion is in order on the nature of the word "success." In the nonprofit world, "success" and "underfunded" are words that can actually go together nicely. In our society, however, success is in many instances equated with acquiring wealth. For an underfunded or even a non-funded nonprofit, though, wealth, by definition, can't be the main criterion of success. If it is for your nonprofit, I'd predict that neither you nor your volunteers will last long. Imparting the way you define success to your volunteers will communicate the value of their work they're doing even as grant applications fail, donations are sparse, the press doesn't care, attendance at your events is barely worth counting, and you're struggling to build a keynote program that will attract sponsorships.

An organization builds its real strength in the dog days. That's when the encouragement to continue derives from the knowledge that you, your officers, and your volunteers are doing great work, meaningful work, necessary work. That somehow, in some way, it will positively impact the future. And this leadership comes from you.

A little while later in this book I'll talk about the importance of having a mission statement that defines what your organization does, how it does it, and who it serves. In the spirit of public service (and you are currently a public benefit corporation), I'd wager that there's little regarding financial success in that mission statement of yours.

Here at the Academic Film Archive of North America (AFA), that's exactly what has kept our volunteers enthusiastic and excited about what we do as an organization and how they're contributing to the success of our mission. We never have more than a few thousands of dollars in the bank (see Chapter 7, "Sponsorships: Building a Definitive,

11

Self-Sustaining, Permanent and Exciting Keynote Program" to see how we got *that*), so obviously we define success in several different ways. I'm going to give you our mission statement, then illustrate how we've been successful in every element. As you craft your own mission statement, it's valuable to consider how you'll quantitatively and qualitatively measure the elements in your mission statement, so you and your officers and volunteers can continually celebrate your wins.

Here's our mission statement. I'll follow it with a breakdown of the key words, with a note about the relative qualitative or quantitative measurement factor associated with each As you read through it, consider how you might apply similar success factors in defining your own organizational objectives: "The mission of The Academic Film Archive of North America is to acquire, preserve, document, and promote academic film by providing an archive, resource, and forum for continuing scholarly advancement and public exhibition."

- Acquire: We currently have more than 5,300 academic films in our archive, with another 2,600 or so held in a private collection that we have access to as an additional resource. That's roughly 8,000 films.
- Preserve: Outside of putting new film leader on prints, we don't have the funds to take poor copies of film, gather all the elements, and create a new one. But we help others that do. One well-known organization, the Archive of the Academy of Motion Picture Arts and Sciences, has used rare prints we have to help make pristine copies of historically significant films.
- Document: In addition to the film notes for hundreds of shows, we've done in public, we have biographies and filmographies of 64 historically significant filmmakers of academic film. We did just about all of it from interviews we conducted.
- Promote: For years, we did weekly public shows at no charge, numbering more than 500 programs. In 2007, looking for a wider audience, we began uploading a selection of our films to the Internet Archive for free viewing. To date we've uploaded nearly 200 films and have had so many views that we can't count them.

- Archive: In addition to having the films themselves, we have a comprehensive database, listing credits, condition, and notes.
- Resource: Our 150-page website is used by scholars, media historians, and the public at large as a resource for academic film.
- Forum: We'd like to do better here. Mostly, our communication is one-way, through the website, and two-way, through e-mail. So far, no one has volunteered to put WordPress up on our website and run a blog.
- Scholarly advancement: When we started our nonprofit, very few people really cared about these films (whole collections were routinely thrown in landfills), but now they're increasingly being investigated by scholars and media historians. Drs. Devin Orgeron and Marsha Gordon have even conducted a graduate class at North Carolina State University on the subject of these films.
- Public exhibition: Our AFA collection at the Internet Archive (http://archive.org/details/academic_films).

Here, I'm not doing this to boast or tell you how wonderful we are. Instead, I'm suggesting that achieving important successes often doesn't have to have anything to do with how successful you are in getting grants. Almost everything involved with the successes we've achieved has been based on volunteering: shows, archival space, website, public exhibition. We started small, doing public shows and handing out flyers on street corners, people started coming, and some of them became important volunteers. And you can achieve significant successes, too, starting small but focused, and having a vision that you believe in so much that you will be able to attract volunteers and keep them motivated.

Many nonprofits are busy trying to keep up with the Joneses, defined as other nonprofits that are able to obtain large grants and perhaps even have a paid staff. The Joneses were in an enviable position until the last recession hit and funders scaled back. Small nonprofits that had made it a habit of practicing sustainability as underfunded organizations rode through it fairly well, while a number of traditionally better-funded nonprofits didn't and closed up shop. The grass isn't always greener, although sometimes it sure can appear to be.

And I guarantee you, sitting around a table with your volunteers and officers at annual meeting time, reeling off your successes for a year, thanking your volunteers and listening to their stories, you'll all have an epiphany that something wonderful, successful, and emotionally embracing has occurred. Your nonprofit successfully accomplished its mission, served the public and was self-sustaining. And it didn't take Big Money to do it.

CHAPTER 2

Don't Quit Your Day Job

As the director of a nonprofit that may be engaged in promoting or preserving an arcane, little-known, misunderstood, and just plain worthwhile subject or service, the reality is that you may never gather enough public funding to pay yourself a salary that will allow you to quit your day job.

Keeping your day job can be beneficial to your organization for a number of reasons. For one, your small but important organization won't fail due to lack of funds to pay salaries. If you're not getting paid a salary, then I'd guess that neither is anybody else in your organization, so you can weather whatever financial challenges come your way. That can be a major factor in keeping your organization sustainable. And you can still eat, pay your rent or mortgage, cover your income taxes, and pay for your health plan. You are financially solvent and not depending on the vagaries of institutional funding to keep your salaried organization afloat. If you've lost your job and are considering forming a nonprofit to support yourself, I strongly suggest you reconsider. Find another job and don't rely on your important nonprofit to pay your personal bills.

Staying away from paying salaries also keeps you away from a number of vexing insurance and accounting obligations that can be so daunting that you'll want to consider their ramifications from the start. They would include directors' and officers' liability coverage, an umbrella policy, workers' compensation, unemployment benefits, Social Security, and payroll taxes. While engaged in a literature search during the writing of this book, I read one book on the subject of forming nonprofits that caused me to question a number of its points, including the suggestion that you add an insurance agent to your board of directors, which seems to me to be a classic example of the fox guarding the hen-house.[1]

Still another good reason to stay employed is that you'll be in a better position to make good decisions based on achieving the success of your nonprofit's mission. That way, you avoid the risk of prioritizing your decisions based on the need to get funding to pay yourself in order to keep your family out of a financial crisis. There are many occasions when idealistically you'll need to place the objectives of your nonprofit's mission over your own immediate wants, and having a steady paycheck that pays the bills can help you over those humps.

So how are you going to manage working a day job and still having the time for your sustainable nonprofit? For one thing, lunches at your day job can take on a whole new level of importance. It's now no longer defined as "downtime." You're now eating a sandwich at your computer and contacting people around the country and throughout the world who link into your passion. You're downloading documents and printing them out so you can read them home at night. And you're cramming new thoughts and ideas into your head until the bell rings and you're back at work again.

That day job really is important. I'm convinced that staying gainfully employed keeps one's life in perspective, as there will be times that your new or existing nonprofit drives you cuckoo and frustrates the heck out of you. Going back to work gives you something else to think about, and another way to be productive, while the issue that's bugging you, nonprofit-wise, chugs along on its own, without your immediate concern. Often, these nonprofit challenges get solved by getting away from things for a bit.

Day-to-Day Operations with No Paid Employees

Assuming that your day job runs eight to five, Monday through Friday, you're going to do some "out of the box" thinking when determining the hours your nonprofit is operating. Take a serious look at why you need a "storefront" and, if you do, when it really needs to be open for visitors. Small museums commonly are only open on weekends, as are some gardens and other botanical operations. Depending on zoning considerations, you may be able to run these out of your home, at least in the beginning. Or do like the founders of a number of other small nonprofits have done and move to a space that has both exhibition space and living quarters. Most small museums I've visited that have evolved from the passions of an entrepreneur actually have living space attached or upstairs. In this category, one that was memorable was Dr. Rampa Rattanarithikul's World Insects and Natural Wonders Museum in Chiang Mai, Thailand, a museum that celebrates the contributions of the mosquito (www.wowasis.com/travelblog/?p= 981).

For years, noncommercial radio stations have been getting by on one part-time employee, the engineer, who is generally available on an on-call basis as needed. Typically in these cases, the board and staff are volunteers and the station runs twenty-four hours a day.

Most, if not all, of your operations, therefore, might occur on nights and weekends. When our organization was in the process of getting launched, we recognized that we needed to accomplish seven things: doing our weekly Thursday night film shows, writing the notes for the shows, e-mailing the notes to the people who would come to our shows (and to the weekly newspaper that gave us film listings), maintaining the website, receiving new films, watching them, then entering them into our film database. Our volunteers were essential to the success of just about all of these operations, and they had full-time jobs, too. Only four of these tasks amounted to things that only I could do: writing film notes, e-mailing, maintaining the website, and entering films in the database. In fact, someone else could have done the e-mailing as well.

Because I couldn't do everything, I was forced to humble myself and ask for help, and that's how we began to put together such an effective volunteer organization. As I discuss later, your volunteers are your most important asset. Having a day job ensures that you'll have to find volunteers, which makes your organization stronger.

A certain amount of flexibility in your day job can be important. On our Board of Officers, two of our volunteers are consultants in the high-tech industry. When they work for one of their clients, it can be a 24/7 situation, in which getting some degree of sleep becomes a real priority. But then there are the client gaps, too, when they may not work for a few days in a row. So a lot of nonprofit "to-dos" that get piled up finally get accomplished in short order during that time. If you or your officers and volunteers are consultants or have flexible work schedules, you're ahead of the game.

I know of a number of folks who are directors of terrific nonprofits and still keep their day jobs. One of them is Jenny Do, a working attorney who is the chairwoman of the Friends of Hue Foundation, an organization she co-founded. Its mission is "dedicated to providing long-term assistance in economic self-sufficiency, health care, education and emergency relief for victims of natural disasters in Thua Thien, Hué, and nearby areas in Central Vietnam" (see her case study in Appendix I). Rick Prelinger, who along with wife Megan Prelinger founded the not-for-profit Prelinger Library in San Francisco (http://www.prelingerlibrary.org) is a university professor. There's a strong precedent, therefore, for working a day job while engaged in operating a nonprofit, and you'll be in good company.

If you currently are operating an underfunded nonprofit that's evaluating whether to fold or merge due to lack of funds, consider instead a move to save it—and its mission—by calling a special board meeting to discuss removing salaried positions and making it all-volunteer. You may lose some people, but perhaps they're worth cutting loose if they don't believe strongly enough in the mission to volunteer, especially if such a move is essential to evolving to a more sustainable operation.

If you're in a start-up situation, recognizing that your nonprofit isn't a replacement for your full-time job can turn your dream of a successful, self-sustaining nonprofit into a reality. A significant start-up expense, namely salaries, has been removed from the equation. So now, if you haven't formally begun to form your nonprofit corporation yet, you're ready to clear off the kitchen table and begin. Let's go to the next chapter.

CHAPTER 3

The First Step: Forming Your Nonprofit Corporation

Although it makes tremendous sense to found a formal nonprofit corporation, you don't have to do that to become a 501(c)(3) nonprofit.[1] Two very good reasons for doing it, though, include having limits on the personal liability of directors, officers, and staff, and many people's belief that you have more credibility as an incorporated organization. Some states, under the Uniform Unincorporated Nonprofit Association Act (UUNAA) or RUUNAA (the revised version), do offer some degree of liability protection for individuals working or volunteering for unincorporated nonprofits.[2] UUNAA was adopted by Alabama, Arkansas, Colorado, Delaware, District of Columbia, Hawaii, Idaho, Louisiana, North Carolina, Texas, West Virginia, Wisconsin, and Wyoming. RUUNAA, which adds elements regarding governance and succession, includes Arkansas, the District of Columbia, Nevada, Iowa, and Pennsylvania and has been introduced for passage in Oklahoma and South Carolina.[3]

Your state's secretary of state will be able to inform you about UUNAA and RUUNA. To find the website for your secretary of state, visit the National Association of Secretaries of State (NASS) website at http://www.nass.org/index.php?option=com_content&view=article&id=44&Itemid=471.

For reasons of liability and credibility, we here at the AFA determined that incorporating was a good idea. Like us, you may also find that going through the process of legally incorporating is one of the most rewarding experiences you'll ever have. You'll hone your mission statement, create your bylaws and articles of incorporation, select your director(s) and officers, and compile your forms for the Internal Revenue

Service. You'll have to create a plan of action, for there are a number of legal steps along the way. And you'll have a formal, legalized record of the manner in which your organization is to run. You don't need to pay anyone to do it for you. Forget about consultants and facilitators—do it yourself.

Let's face it, doing it all that way will at first seem a daunting task. You're a person with a passion and a vision and probably not a lawyer or a tax attorney. You'll want step-by-step instructions for obtaining a federal 501(c)(3) tax exemption and qualifying for public charity status with the IRS. For this reason, I strongly recommend picking up a copy of attorney Anthony Mancuso's book *How to Form a Nonprofit Corporation* published by Nolo Press (www.nolo.com).[4] When I formed the AFA, I went cover-to-cover in that book, using his guidelines to draw up bylaws, articles of incorporation, and the IRS tax-exemption application. Many of the forms you'll need are in Mancuso's book or are available from the Nolo Press website. This 330-page book contains easy-to-understand legal advice and facilitates the hands-on process of creating your nonprofit. You'll need to be aware of laws and regulations relating to nonprofits, and you'll find Mancuso's book helpful, even if you have a lawyer or a tax attorney on your team. One issue Mancuso discusses that I found especially helpful was whether or not to form a membership corporation. There are several good reasons not to. If you do become a membership organization, it will impact the terminology you'll be using in your Articles of Incorporation and Bylaws. In my opinion, using Mancuso's book to assist you in forming your nonprofit can save you a significant amount of time.

There are some important legal issues that should be addressed, though, as well as non-legal ones that Mancuso doesn't cover. And these should be considered as you go forward (later, I provide a time line of how long you can reasonably expect to have to wait to have your state and federal applications approved). These include creating a mission statement, acquiring a URL (a Uniform Resource Locator, better known as a web address) that conforms to your corporate name, creating a compelling logo, and putting some serious thought into the number of people you put on your board. But first, let's take a cursory look at what makes a 501(c)(3).

So What's a 501(c)(3)?

The IRS has classified the 501(c)(3) category in an operational test, as element 7.25.3.4 (02–23–1999) in part 7 ("Rulings and Agreements") of the Internal Revenue Manual, as follows[5]:

1. To satisfy the operational test, an organization must be operated exclusively for one or more of the following purposes:
   - religious
   - charitable
   - scientific
   - testing for public safety
   - literary
   - educational
   - fostering national or international sports competition (but only if no part of its activities involves the provision of athletic facilities or equipment)
   - prevention of cruelty to children or animals

As such, organizations that conform to the operational test and are qualified by the IRS under 501(c)(3) may claim exempt status under federal and state tax laws. They may also receive tax-deductible contributions from donors and are eligible for benefits that do not apply to various other nonprofits in other tax-exempt categories.

You'll notice that the IRS uses the word "exclusively." That means that your nonprofit cannot be at cross-purposes with itself, and in both the spirit and the letter of the law it emphasizes that making a profit cannot be your major corporate objective. If I were forming a nonprofit based on Rafflesia, the ichigenkin, or glass insulators, I might therefore take a serious look at forming my organization under the "educational" category and develop my mission statement and overall objectives accordingly. Let's now look at some elements essential to you as you begin to create your nonprofit corporation.

As a publicly supported charity, you will have to solicit funding from the general community as well as occasional grants from public agencies. If one or two large benefactors, for example, provide the lion's share of your support, then the IRS may deny you public charity status. The IRS mandates that more than one-third of an organization's support must come from "contributions, membership fees, and gross receipts from activities related to its exempt functions."[6] There is a significant body of law relating to what exactly constitutes a public charity, another important element being that you must continually attract government or public support. A good way to do this is to ensure that you have an ongoing program for soliciting money from the public or governmental agencies (see Chapter 7, "Sponsorships: Building a Definitive, Self-Sustaining, Permanent and Exciting Keynote Program").[7]

Creating a Mission Statement

Initially, you should request information and forms from your secretary of state so you can begin the process of filing your Articles of Incorporation. You'll need to have a formalized mission statement (which may also be called a "statement of purpose" or something similar) to apply for nonprofit status, and it will serve as a basic guideline of what objectives your organization seeks to accomplish. Consider these questions: *What* are you promoting? *How* are you doing it? *What* resources are you offering? *Whom* will it serve? *What* are its goals? Once you have answers to these questions, try to create a powerful one-sentence mission statement, using a few choice verbs and nouns and stating whom you will serve.

While crafting your mission statement, in addition to your organization's overall goals, think of some concrete, measureable objectives that, when met, will be indicators that your nonprofit has achieved success in those areas. For example, one element in our mission statement is "public exhibition" of films in our archive. How do we measure that? We take attendance figures at our screenings, and our Internet Archive statistics tell us the number of people who have viewed our online films.

You were introduced to the AFA's mission statement in the last chapter, and you can use it as a partial template when you create yours. Ours is on the home page of our website and also on the reverse sides of our business cards, and I'd recommend that you do that as well. This is it again: "The mission of The Academic Film Archive of North America is to acquire, preserve, document, and promote academic film by providing an archive, resource, and forum for continuing scholarly advancement and public exhibition."

Let's pull it apart grammatically. The object is "academic film." The verbs are "acquire," "preserve," "document," and "promote," and the gerund is "providing." What we provide consists of the nouns "archive," "resource," and "forum." And those we serve are encompassed in "scholarly advancement" and "public exhibition." To date, everything we've ever done to date is described in that mission statement, and I think it pretty well covers the future, too.

You can use our formula as a model. You may have to agonize over it a bit, but do try to complete it in one sentence. Forget about paying a facilitator to assist you. Instead, test it out on your friends and colleagues, encourage them to be critical, listen to their ideas, and revise, revise, revise. What you'll end up with should be a mission statement with a marketing and publicity element to it. Funding is always a challenge, and your mission statement should show a clarity of vision and thought that will add to your business professionalism when you engage in communicating with people and organizations that might be amenable to giving you some funding.

Essentially, a short, easy-to-understand mission statement will become your "elevator pitch," so you can easily and comprehensively describe what your organization does, to anyone who asks. As I mentioned earlier, putting your mission statement on the reverse side of your business card is a very good idea, as you can then show it to anyone who might be interested. That's why one sentence is best. You want people to "get it" right away. A later chapter of this book, "Crafting a Succession Plan: Leaving a Legacy and Documenting Your Assets," further discusses your mission statement from the perspective of how effective you've been in meeting its stated objectives.

Naming Your Organization and Buying a Web URL That Relates to It

If you haven't yet done so, you will need to choose a corporate name that is unique in terms of any other corporation doing business in your state and isn't confusable with those others. Once you come up with one, do an Internet search to see if there are any similar to yours. WhoIs (www.whois.com) and Vox Domains (www.voxdomains.

com) are two resources for performing a name search (they provide web development, hosting, and e-mail options, as well). If your name is already taken, re-craft and search again. This is important, for if your secretary of state determines that your corporate name is too similar to another on the registered list, your Articles of Incorporation application will be returned to you without approval. There are, in addition, trademarks to consider, so try to ensure that your corporate name doesn't infringe on a trade name or trademark. The United States Trademark and Patent Office offers a trademark search system (TESS) at http://tess2.uspto.gov/bin/gate.exe?f=tess&state=4803:29avj9.1.1. I recommend that you make a real effort to find a name that is truly unique and yet adequately describes what your nonprofit does. In our case, for example, we originally wanted to call our organization the "Academic Film Archive," but we soon realized it was too similar to the already-existing "Academy Film Archive," which is part of the very well-known "Academy of Motion Picture Arts and Sciences." So we renamed our organization to the more descriptive "Academic Film Archive of North America," and our application was successful. Your state may provide you with a number of options to search and even hold a name while you're going through the application process. The State of California, for example, allows you to check for name availability (by snail mail only), reserve a name for sixty days (for a fee, again by snail mail only), and even reserve it by phone ($100 deposit).[8] We did none of that and instead came up with a name that was unique enough so that nothing close to it came up on an Internet search. We went with it, bought a URL, and filed our Articles of Incorporation.

In naming your organization, you should give some thought to having a web URL that will make sense in terms of the corporate name you use. As discussed in the previous paragraph, begin by putting together a list with suggestions of several corporate names that would work for you. The experience we had here at the AFA is again illustrative. We specialize in archiving and documenting the history of classroom educational films but found that using the names "education" and "educational" was problematic from several perspectives. There appeared to be thousands of organizations and schools using those words, and we couldn't find a corporate name we liked that used them and still had an available URL. So instead of calling our collection "educational films"—words that also seemed a bit pedantic and nondescriptive to us—we called them "academic." We thus started with the term "Academic Film Archive." As mentioned earlier, we were likewise concerned about the similarity of our name to that of a different organization. In addition, we found that both the "www.afa.org" and "www. afa.com" URLs were already taken. Since many of the films we've championed were made by the National Film Board of Canada, we thought it appropriate that our corporate name reflect the fact that we weren't solely occupied with films created in the United States, and thus the "Academic Film Archive of North America" made sense. And "www. afana.org" was an available URL, so we bought it immediately.

As you can see, the process of naming your organization to conform to an available URL can subtly change your mission statement, your definition of your organization's expertise, and even your publicity. And having done that, you may find, as we did, that you'll begin changing public discourse to incorporate your new definitions. Buying a URL is inexpensive, as low as $8 as of this writing, and we've found that URLs that are here today are often bought tomorrow. So if you're reasonably sure you've come up with a unique name, secure the URL right away, just in case.

How Many Directors Should You Have on Your Board? How About Only One?

Depending on the state in which you incorporate, you may have the option of having only one director. One big advantage of having yourself as the only director is that your vision and organization cannot be hijacked by a board voting you off the team. Another is that you lower the risk of having your meetings taken over by nonproductive discussions involving minutiae, one of the banes of noncommercial radio meetings, in particular. This can occur in other nonprofits, too. In the chapter on volunteers, I mention how the Eagle Scouts contributed to our organization through a shelving project. This occurred during the scouts' gay controversy (as discussed later), and I can just imagine the endless, endless discussions that other boards may well have had as to whether this was a group with whom they wanted to work, philosophically speaking. Long-winded pontifications and discourses are endemic to nonprofits (particularly, I fear, to those here in the San Francisco Bay Area). I've witnessed numbers of them in several nonprofits. They can take hours, and often nothing is accomplished except an agreement that "we'll agree to disagree," at which point everyone is so burned out that they all go home frustrated, without having addressed more important items on the agenda. With only one director, timely decisions can move forward unilaterally regarding projects that are critically important, while discussions not directly concerning the mission of the organization can take place at venues other than your formal meetings.

Another concern I had while forming the AFA was that other potential voting board members, seeing a pot of grant gold at the end of a hypothetical rainbow, might change the focus away from academic classroom film and instead shift to a cinematic genre that might produce more income or publicity. Documentary, experimental, and home movies were just three of many non-academic film-specific directions that I was concerned about. The "grass is greener" syndrome can potentially divide a nonprofit and cause it to change direction radically away from its original mission. Discussions with other team members can be vitally important, though, and can help you, as the sole director, to make well-thought-out decisions. As Audrey Wong, Grants Manager of Silicon Valley Creates, notes, having checks and balances in your organization can be critical to ensuring that your organization ship stays on-course.[9]

So let's say you incorporate in a state that allows you to have only one board member (you). How do you give people positions of responsibility without making them voting members? You create a Board of Officers. You can give each of them authority, responsibility, and a title. You can also allow them to vote on anything they like, but the results, of course, are not formally binding. There are times, certainly, when you'll want them to vote in an advisory capacity. In our case, every financial decision is made with the advice of our Chief Financial Officer (CFO) and major decisions are discussed thoroughly at the meetings of our Board of Officers.

Then again, if you're located in a state in which you do have to have more than one board member, ensure that each potential candidate is in complete alignment with your mission statement. Jim Reed,

Curator of Archives and Library at History San José, lists three important points of consideration from his own experience:

- If you get businesspeople or attorneys on boards, their first thought is "this organization should be run like a business." *Wrong*. A business exists to make money; a nonprofit exists to provide a service. This is not to say that some business practices aren't appropriate in nonprofits, but it's too easy for the tail to end up wagging the dog.
- I dealt with one board in St. Louis where the individuals used fund-raising events to pay off their social debts and didn't care if any money was raised.
- Boards should *advise* on policy, monitor the finances, and raise money. All other activities are secondary to that.

Differing from Jim somewhat on the first point, I do believe that sound business practices are a key factor in maintaining a sustainable nonprofit. Paying bills on time, for instance, virtually guarantees that you won't be behind an ever-moving financial eight ball. As Audrey Wong states, nonprofits "should run like a responsible business which manages itself so well that it can provide service or products."[10] In terms of general business practices, I'd also be remiss if I didn't mention one nonprofit that had a board member who refused to bathe. Soon after he was added to the board, people stopped coming to meetings. Within a year volunteerism had shrunk, and a year later the nonprofit was effectively defunct. For any potential candidate, I recommend that you meet the individual informally at a public venue two or three times first to ensure that his or her social habits are at least at a minimum level of acceptance.

In California, where we incorporated, a director can serve for a term of up to six years. In the bylaws, I added that there would be no limit to the number of successive terms a director could serve, thus helping to preserve the original purpose of our organization. When we applied for nonprofit status, the following states offered the option of having a single director, with no residency requirements: California, Colorado, Delaware, Georgia, Iowa, Kansas, Michigan, Mississippi, Nevada, North Carolina, Oklahoma, Oregon, Pennsylvania, Virginia, Washington, and West Virginia.

The vast majority of nonprofits have more than one director. Some actually sell the seats on a yearly basis (one of our local museums charges $40,000 each year) or have implemented a similar "give, get, or get off" policy associated with contributing or raising a set amount. You do want to have other people involved in the inner workings of your organization, but there are perils in having a formal board of directors that might easily cause the organization to veer in a direction that could potentially contribute to its demise. As Jim Reed notes, "There is an all-too-frequent pattern of founders of nonprofits being driven from their jobs by the governing Board within a few years of the organization being established."[11]

To this last point, here's a story worth considering: An individual well-known for starting and running nonprofit media outlets moved into a new city, helped create a nonprofit organization and set up the board of directors. He worked on putting a team together to build the entity, contributed thousands of dollars' worth of resource material, bought the property on which the media outlet would exist, and lent the nonprofit several hundred thousand dollars to get everything rolling.

Feeling he was no longer worth having around, the board voted him off. Effectively, he was fired. He was accused of putting the organization in debt, among other things. The board wasn't even vaguely grateful for the time, work, and money he'd put into it. They just wanted him out. What did he do? He called in the debt, sold the property on which the nonprofit was located and left town. Within a couple of years, the media outlet was defunct. This wasn't the first time a founder has been expelled from the board of directors and it won't be the last. In this case, that decision ultimately caused the organization to fold.

If you do elect to have multiple voting members on your board or are incorporating in a state that mandates it, vet your potential officers first, then choose very carefully. You'll also want to stagger terms so that your board doesn't have a complete overhaul when terms end. A good method, for example is to have several positions terminate after two years, several more after three, for example. Then make subsequent terms two-year positions. Personal relationships among board members can be a blessing ... or a curse. Think having your spouse on the board is a good idea? It may or may not be, so do think it through thoroughly. Before making final choices, you'll want to vet your potential board officers to determine how maturely and effectively they operate in a group. I recommend having a few informal meetings before you file your Articles of Incorporation so you can see how people behave and what their agendas seem to be. Discuss your mission statement and the goals and objectives of your organization, and work out both what your organization will do and, at least as important, what it won't do. One possible bone of contention you'll want to bring up in at least once is the subject of paid employees, now or in the future. And that should include directors and officers. If several potential board choices are emphatically all for volunteers while others want to begin with at least one paid position, it would be better to reach an agreement about how this will be handled before you formally choose your members. If it's at all possible, create a board that will work together to achieve commonly agreed goals and methods of operation. Initial disagreement on major issues should be seen as a red flag. Constructive dissention can be a good thing in a nonprofit, but you should determine both the different tasks and professional demeanor you desire. You may want to identify individuals as being best effective as either voting board directors or nonvoting ones and build your organization accordingly.

Limiting the Number of Directors to Avoid Meeting Fatigue

Nonprofit radio stations are a good example of the problems associated with "meeting fatigue." They tend toward board meetings that seem to go on endlessly and at all-too-frequent intervals on the subject of programming. Everyone does have a strong opinion, and it's often hard to gain agreement on what should and should not go on the air. One noncommercial station I know of (and there are probably many more) had an ongoing series of meetings to determine whether rock and roll should be played, with one faction declaring that it was far too commercial and the other decrying the loss of freedom if on-air personnel couldn't play what they wanted to. In such situations, zealots on either side can effectively take over a meeting, making it a painful experience for others supporting more measured approaches. In a one-director operation, such discussions can be tabled or sent to a committee. In those having multiple voting board members, meeting fatigue may well drive good people away from the board. This goes back to the importance of having a strong mission statement. Think ahead to what topics might cause meetings to become derailed, fix them at the front end, and embed that information in your mission statement.

Filing Your Articles of Incorporation

Once you've chosen your name, you'll want to file Articles of Incorporation with your secretary of state. This is your first important legal step, for you'll need to be incorporated as a nonprofit in order to file your subsequent applications with the IRS. This is a relatively simple document, and as the following time line suggests, you could receive approval in a very short period of time (ours was two weeks). In the state of California, where we filed, it encompassed six items, as simplified below. Depending on your state and the structure of your organization, it might differ from ours, but this represents typical requirements.

1. Name of the corporation
2. Agreement that it is being organized under Nonprofit Benefit Corporation Law and a simple statement indicating the purpose of the organization
3. The name and address of the corporation's initial agent for service of process
4. An agreement that the corporation is organized for public purposes within the meaning of section 501(c)(3) of the Internal Revenue Service Code, will keep its activities within that statute, will not attempt to influence legislation, and will avoid participation or intervention in any political campaign
5. The name(s) and address(es) of the initial director(s) of the organization
6. An agreement that no individual associated with the organization will derive personal benefit from the net income or assets of the

corporation and, should the corporation dissolve, assets will be distributed to organizations described under section 501(c)(3)

Obtaining an Employer Identification Number (EIN) from the Internal Revenue Service

You will need a valid EIN associated with your corporation when you file your Form 1023. Obtaining an EIN is easy, and you can apply for it by telephone from the IRS at (800) 829–4933 or online.[12]

Creating Your Bylaws

Your bylaws contain the instructions you use to operate your organization. They include data on your office(s), nonprofit purposes, and information on your director(s), including powers, duties, term of office, and compensation. Bylaws also include data on meetings: where they're conducted, how often, quorum, and conduct. There are also sections relating to liability, indemnification, insurance, and duties, qualifications of officers, and a number of other important items particular to how your operation is run. I really enjoyed the process of creating our bylaws, as it caused me to think through how our operation could be run most efficiently, effectively, and legally. Audrey Wong has some practical advice that you should bear in mind:

> These are by-**laws** that you create for yourselves, but you have to stick to them. So be careful [as to how] you craft them. Do so in a deliberate, thoughtful, and practical way that won't require you to revise them if you find they don't work out. E.g., don't set numbers on board meetings or quorum level too high. You can always call more meetings or have more board members—but if you have fewer than you stated in your bylaws, then you are out of compliance.[13]

My recommendation is that you think in terms of organizational transparency and be public about the way your nonprofit is set up. A good method of initiating transparency is to post your bylaws on your website, as we did (http://www.afana.org/bylaws.htm). In creating effective bylaws, you don't have to reinvent the wheel. I found the most effective manner of creating ours was by starting with the boilerplate in Anthony Mancuso's book.[14]

Completing IRS Form 1023

You're going to spend a certain amount of time completing your Application for Recognition of Exemption Under section 501(c)(3) of the Internal Revenue Code, but it's an important and rewarding part of the process. The application includes Form 1023 and instructions, Form 872-C (Consent Fixing Period of Limitation Upon Assessment of Tax Under Section 4940 of the Internal Revenue Code), and Form 8718 (User Fee for Exempt Organization Determination Letter Request).

Form 1023 is comprehensive and takes time to complete. The IRS recognizes this, and has published a document estimating the time needed to complete the application, divided into sections corresponding to Record Keeping, Learning About the Law, Preparing the Form, and Copying, Assembling, and Sending it (http://www.irs.gov/instruc tions/i1023/ar02.html). It's a reliable indicator of the time involved and very much worth reading.

Part 4 of the 1023 requires financial data entry, so if you haven't yet designated a CFO/Treasurer, now's the time to do it, so the person chosen can begin compiling the financial data you'll need for your 1023 form (see the chapter on volunteers in this book for more on the CFO position).

Dressed for Success: Your IRS Acceptance and Final Determination Letters

When the IRS determines that you make a good candidate for tax-exempt status, it will issue you an advance ruling acceptance letter that will allow you to operate as a nonprofit for a period of five years. After that time passes, the IRS will review your operation and if it determines that you've acted properly within the law you will receive a final determination letter.

The advance ruling and final determination letters allow you to function as a nonprofit and you'll need to show your most current IRS letter to most funders. We've found that an easy way to confirm to other parties that we're a valid 501(c)(3) is to post a PDF of it on our website. Ours is at http://www.afana.org/501c3.htm.

Critical Forms and Time Lines

How long does it take to get your nonprofit formally approved and all the paperwork signed off? I went through our corporate records book and have listed here all the forms we filled out, the dates of submission (when available) and the date of acceptance. Bear in mind that this occurred more than ten years ago (2001–2002), so your own time line may be different. It may also vary depending on the state in which you're filing.

- State of California Articles of Incorporation sent to the secretary of state, February 22, 2001
- State of California Articles of Incorporation endorsed and filed by the state, March 5, 2001
- State of California Franchise Tax Board state tax exemption acceptance letter received, dated July 12, 2001
- IRS Form 1023 Application for Recognition of Exemption application sent to IRS September 4, 2001
- IRS Form 8718 User Fee for Exempt Organization Determination Letter Request sent to IRS September 4, 2001
- IRS acknowledgement of request for exemption from federal income tax letter received, dated September 14, 2001
- IRS Form 872-C Consent Fixing Period of Limitation sent to IRS September 4, 2001; IRS acknowledgement stamped October 2, 2001
- IRS advance ruling acceptance letter received, stamped October 2, 2001
- IRS final determination letter received, stamped June 24, 2006

What is apparent in reviewing these stages is just how quickly things move from the date you file your Articles of Incorporation to the time you receive your advance ruling acceptance letter from the IRS. In our case, it took a little over seven months. Depending on how your organization is created, you may have to file other forms as well (again, I refer you to Mancuso's book), but those listed here are the milestones. When you finally receive your IRS advance ruling acceptance letter, you're really in business.

So now that you are indeed in business, the next chapter will start you thinking about how you'll put together all the things you'll need to get your formal office up and running.

Creating a Compelling Logo and Crafting Your Letterhead and Brochure

There's a lot of value in putting some time into creating a logo that will fit your name and purpose. But don't make it pedestrian. If you're not a graphics designer, we'd suggest you conceptualize what your great logo would look like, then make a few sketches and select the colors. Once you've done this, you can hire a graphics designer to execute it for you. Your new logo will be on your website, business cards, correspondence, and publicity items. It does not necessarily have to contain your entire corporate name.

That's how we did it. We wanted it to be simple and film related. "AFANA" was too long, we thought, so shortened the whole thing to "AFA." We then created three boxes, each containing one of those three letters, intending them to be reminiscent of the countdown numbers in revolving circles that you sometimes see before a film begins. The "movement" in our logo is created by changing the colors on different parts of each of the three "wheels." We knew we'd need to occasionally print our logo in black and white (see the note on letterhead and stationery later), so the colors we selected had to register well when transformed for those applications. We wanted large and small versions, and jpegs for Internet and e-mail use as well. Since none of us were graphics designers, our volunteer Rob McGlynn directed us to designer Joe Sikoryak, who created a wonderful graphic in all iterations and was good enough to donate it to the cause. In-kind donations of this sort will be addressed later, but this is a good example of why, early in the life of your organization, you'll want to think in terms of people who can help you in return for a tax deduction.

Creating a mission statement, developing a corporate name, buying a URL, and designing a logo all go hand in hand, so consider multitasking and working on them all at the same time.

Eventually, you'll use your logo on your letterhead. As a cost-saving measure, instead of printing a formal letterhead you can create a template in your word-processing program with your logo at the top. Our template letterhead includes contact information, our Employer Identification Number (EIN), our 501(c)(3) designation, and our mission statement at the bottom. We type the text for each letter right into the template. Even though our logo is in full color, we elect to print all letters on our black-and-white laser printer, another way to avoid the costs associated with using a color printer. Another good reason for using a word-processing template is that you can always change anything easily, including any eventual change of address, without having to toss out your printed stationery and buy it anew.

Black and white is how we chose to go on our brochure, too, which describes what our organization does, whom it serves, and includes four photos as well as a very brief request for donations. For this we did go to a print shop and made it on 8½ × 11-inch glossy card stock, which folds into thirds when we put it in an envelope. We also went to a print shop for our standard #10 envelopes but elected not to include a return address, since we knew we might be moving and didn't want to toss out our envelopes when we did. Instead, we again used our office black-and-white laser printer to create labels that we affix to the backs of the envelope when we send mail.

Checklist of Important Milestones

- Create a mission statement.
- Request a nonprofit application packet from your secretary of state.
- Name your organization and buy a web URL that relates to it.
- Determine the number of directors you'll have on your board.
- Submit and receive approval for your Articles of Incorporation.

- Obtain an Employer Identification Number (EIN) from the Internal Revenue Service.
- Apply and receive approval for tax-exempt status from your state tax agency.
- Write your bylaws.
- Apply and receive approval from the IRS for Recognition of Exemption under Section 501(c)(3) of the Internal Revenue Code (Forms 1023 and 872-C). Submit User Fee for Exempt Organization Determination Letter Request (Form 8718) in the same packet.
- Create a compelling logo and design your letterhead.

Chapter 4

Setting Up Your Sustainable Nonprofit Office

Your biggest expense may conceivably be in setting up your office. The good news is that you probably already have a lot of the equipment, tools, and software that you need. You can also buy used materials, and when you finally get your IRS Employer Identification number under section 501(c)(3) of the Internal Revenue Code, a number of amazing options will become available to you, including greatly discounted software, at TechSoup.org (see "Viva TechSoup!" later in this chapter). You should also seriously give some consideration to housing your operation in donated space.

Do You Really Need to Pay Rent?

As you're setting up your nonprofit, you may want to consider if it's worthwhile paying rent. And if your underfunded nonprofit is already paying rent, might it be worthwhile to reconsider? Many nonprofits have an office set up in the home of a director or officer (see the case studies in Appendix I). This is an ideal situation if you don't get a lot of "walk-ins" and really just use the office for administrative purposes. In addition to avoiding rent, there are a number of insurance costs with which you probably don't need to bother. You will have to make certain records available for public inspection. If you do need to meet someone, you can always go to that person's office or meet at a coffee shop. You can also photocopy and mail requested public documents to the individual asking for them or make PDFs and e-mail them.

In addition to your office, you may need space to house a collection, which is important if your nonprofit is a museum, archive, or library. Whether it's an office, a collection space, or even an event location, I encourage you to meet with other organizations in your area to see if they will donate or share ongoing space with you. These can be either businesses or other nonprofits. If it's a business, it may be able to deduct your presence as an in-kind donation. For donated space, you may have to sign a waiver stating that the donor bears no responsibility for anything that may happen to your assets, including theft, fire, and water damage. I think this is a pretty good trade-off. You may also want to think about the insurance aspect, to either cover your assets or consider what may happen if someone trips and falls while entering your donated space. If the latter, you may find that the space is already insured for that possibility and you may or may not need an amendment to the insured's policy.

Here at the AFA, we've never paid rent in our more than a decade of existence. That includes both venues for our public shows as well as the space in which our collection is held. Here's how we do it. Our administrative office is home based, as is our CFO's office. Our film collection is stored at History San José (and yes, we signed an indemnification letter with them). Whenever we have events and benefits, the space is donated (see the chapter "Events, Benefits, Conferences and Nontraditional Ways to Pay a Few Bills" for more on this). We also use "virtual space" on the Internet to show our films, which has become the major public presence of our organization. They're hosted on the Internet Archive (see the chapter "Sponsorships: Building a Definitive, Self-Sustaining, Permanent and Exciting Keynote Program") and we don't pay rent there, either.

So go ahead and strongly think though the idea of what you really need in terms of space rental. Think critically, with an eye toward sustainability. In many cases, nonprofits can do it the same way we did, with modifications based on the particulars of the given organization.

Do You Really Need a Dedicated Phone Line?

In some circumstances, you may not need a landline, especially in initially forming your organization. For example, let's say you already run a home-based, sole-proprietor business and are just starting your nonprofit. That means you'll have two operations using one phone line. When you pick up, instead of answering with either organization's name, just say, "Good afternoon, this is [your name]." For your outgoing voice-mail message, again, it's, "Hi, this is [your name]. Please leave a message at the sound of the tone." History San José's Jim Reed adds a cautionary note that some telephone service providers can be "picky" about this and demand that you buy a separate business line, so you might want to be aware of your local provider's provisos as you move forward. In the chapter "The First Step: Forming Your Nonprofit Corporation," I discussed the value of creating your letterhead as a template on your word processor and printing on-demand, rather than paying a printer for stationery. If you do this, you won't have to worry about the printing costs associated with changing your phone number on preprinted documents, should that eventuality arise.

So what hardware, software, and web options will you *really* need for your office?

Office Hardware, Software, and Web Options

Before going out and buying anything, ask your officers, volunteers, and friends if they have any hardware or software that they'd be willing to donate. Once you're a bona fide nonprofit, you can also make calls to other nonprofits and ask if they have any hardware or software they'll soon be deaccessioning. By law, they can legally transfer it to another nonprofit. If you're good at finding donors, you may find that there is very little you'll have to purchase in the way of equipment. When we set up our office at the AFA, we had most of what we needed donated by volunteers. In addition, we acquired some important software when a local nonprofit dissolved its organization and had to transfer assets to another nonprofit. We also acquired new software and hardware that was donated by businesses. How did we find that source? From company employees who were also volunteers of ours. In some cases, they asked about equipment that was going to be replaced. It was donated to us and the business got a tax write-off. To sum up, your best resources for free equipment are your officers and volunteers, businesses, other nonprofits, and dissolved nonprofits.

If you have to buy software, I'm a real believer in acquiring what's known as commercial off-the-shelf (COTS) software, as opposed to hiring programmers to build custom programs based on products with which they're familiar. As I mention later, TechSoup.org will, in most cases, be the least expensive way for you to acquire commercially available software. If you're thinking of designing your own software or having someone do it for you, I urge you to reconsider. Authors David J. Neff and Randal C. Moss[1] describe some of the issues that tend to come up between programmers and information technology (IT) staff, so we at the AFA don't use anything—-hardware or software—that requires a programmer or an IT person. The only software we used that could have potentially required a programmer was related to either our website or our collections database. For the former we used a commercial product (Microsoft FrontPage) that allowed us to put up a site without having to write code, and for the latter we figured out how to design our fields in one day using Microsoft Access (see "Spreadsheet Software" later in this chapter). As will be discussed later, having to pay maintenance fees for ongoing programming or updating, an especially common practice with websites, is something you'll want to avoid.

Increasingly, information that has traditionally been kept on local computers or servers is moving to remote servers on the Internet. This is known as SaaS (Software as a Service) or simply as "the cloud." You do have a choice, and you can adopt either approach for virtually any of the software applications discussed here. The pros and cons are fairly simple to understand. If you host the software on your own computer or server, you typically own the software outright, control your own software security through your Internet security software, and must be responsible for performing your own backups. Cloud-based applications do all of that for you but charge you a monthly or yearly fee for the service. Which should you choose? We like owning our own software, which we think controls costs more effectively. The negative aspect is that we do have to remember to back up everything on a regular basis.

It's extremely important, as you're adding hardware, software, and Internet resources to your office, to compile an "Access and Assets" document, which is addressed in the "Crafting a Succession Plan: Leaving a Legacy and Documenting Your Assets" later in this book. If you fail to document your access and assets information and keep it current, please reflect for a moment on how anyone succeeding you or a member of your data team will know where everything is and how to access it.

What Do You Need for Your Office?

Here at the AFA, we've standardized on Wintel (Windows-Intel) PCs, rather than Apple products, so some of the items mentioned in this chapter will be specific to that technology. If you're an Apple person, don't fret, as there are Apple-specific products that will do much of the same thing. So here goes. Let's set up your office.

Hardware Necessities

COMPUTER

You'll need a computer, of course, and we like doing everything initially on a desktop PC with a hard drive with lots of storage and a CD/DVD drive. Many people and organizations send us material on CDs and DVDs, and we need the drive to load that material into our computer. If your desktop PC doesn't have that capability, you can buy a USB-based drive that you can add to your system for about $100.

We also use a notebook (or a laptop) computer, and we load our CRM (Customer Relationship Management) database and films database software onto it. That way, when we're on the road or at our film archive everything we need from our office desktop is right there, at our fingertips.

PRINTER AND SCANNER

I recommend getting a scanner, as you'll probably be copying materials, from books to documents to photographs. I recommend acquiring a low-cost black-and-white laser printer. You can find black-and-white laser printers used, in the marketplace, and a big advantage is that consumable costs (standard paper and toner cartridges) are low.

For our purposes, we consider color inkjet printers a luxury, not a necessity. Even our letterhead prints out as black and white.

You probably do not need a facsimile machine. The proliferation of junk faxes caused a significant number of businesses to instead opt for sending documents as e-mail attachments. For documents that you do not originate, use your scanner and save them as word processor documents and/or acquire software that will allow you to create a PDF (Portable Document Format). See more on PDFs in "PDF Solutions" later in this chapter.

USB Backup Hard Drive and Web Backup

You'll want to back up the data on your computer on an ongoing basis as a means of disaster recovery. For this, a hardware option you'll want to consider is a USB-connected backup hard drive, which costs around $80 in today's market for a one- or two-terabyte drive. I'd recommend two drives, which allows you to alternately switch from one to another, and that way you always have a backup drive that's more current than the other one. Do locate your backup drives at a space physically away from your office, just in case real disaster hits. In California, for example, we're prone to earthquakes, so it makes sense to store the backup drives in another building a few feet away, just in case.

You can also subscribe to a cloud-based backup utility instead of doing it yourself on a separate hard drive. Doing it via the cloud may be more expensive due to subscription fees, with the advantage that it's automated, and you won't have to remember to do it on an ongoing basis. For more on this option, see "Backup Software and Web-based Backup," later in this chapter.

That does it for hardware, just a PC, printer and scanner, backup drive and perhaps a secondary laptop or notebook computer. Start simply and inexpensively.

Software and Internet Necessities and Resources

Increasingly, many organizations are utilizing office tools available on the Internet, rather than hosting software on their own computers. The discussion of software products here, therefore, would include those found on the Internet. Whichever method you use, you will have to document user names, passwords, and various identification numbers. You can do this manually or through software or Internet resources such as Password Vault Manager (http://passwordvaultmana ger).

WORD PROCESSOR AND OCR SOFTWARE

A word-processing program such as Microsoft Word is a must. And along with that, you should strongly consider OCR (optical character recognition) software that will allow you to scan documents and convert scanned text to something readable that you can then transfer to your word processor program. If you're going to be doing a lot of writing for your website, chances are that you'll occasionally want to quote from a source in a book that you can scan. That's where OCR software comes in handy. The good news is that OCR software often comes embedded in the software that comes with your scanner. Our HP scanner has a terrific OCR program that does it all. There are also OCR products on the market, including ABBYY FineReader (www. abbyy.com).

PDF SOLUTIONS

Adobe's PDF (Portable Document Format) has become the de facto standard for sending documents by e-mail that were formerly sent by fax. Adobe makes the PDF reader available free of charge (http://get.adobe.com/reader), but you still have to have a utility that will create PDFs. The good news is that your scanner software may already have such a utility that will enable you to create a PDF when you scan and save a document. Microsoft Word offers this utility as well when you access the "save as" feature. Adobe Acrobat (www.adobe. com/products) is a stand-alone product that will create PDFs if you don't already have this utility. A highly recommended free PDF product is PDFCreator (http://www.pdfforge.org/pdfcreator). Once you download it, it attaches to various programs that will allow you to create PDFs from them. As an example, we sometimes have to e-mail invoices for sponsorships that were created in our financial software, and our software's e-mail interface is troublesome. Rather than printing the invoice, scanning it, saving it, and e-mailing it, using PDFCreator allows us to save the invoice directly as a print function. We then e-mail it as a file. This saves us the time of printing and scanning it.

SPREADSHEET SOFTWARE

There may be a number of times that you'll want to put data into a spreadsheet. We, for instance, log our sponsored Save A Film donations there, so we see at a glance the name of a given sponsored film, the date we received the donation, who made the donation, and the shipping dates to and from our digitizer. We also log permission dates received from copyright holders. We use Microsoft Excel. If you have a collection of materials, you may be initially keeping its documentation on a spreadsheet. In time, this may become cumbersome, so I recommend acquiring a separate database collections software program like PastPerfect (moderately customizable) or Microsoft Access (fully customizable). See "Collections Database Software" later in this chapter.

CRM DATABASE SOLUTIONS

You will want to have a CRM (Customer/Constituency Relationship Management) database, to keep track of people, companies, and organizations that are important to you. Rolodexes are things of the past, CRMs are quick at searching for your contacts, and you can insert conversational items in the "notes" field. You can either adopt a solution that's hosted on your own internal server or subscribe to one operating as a SaaS online product. With an eye to sustainability, we prefer using a CRM that is resident on our desktop PC but can be instantly transferred to our notebook computer when we're in the field. One product that does this nicely is Swiftpage's ACT! Pro (www.act.com), but there are others. FileMaker Pro (www.filemaker.com) is a product that was originally built for Apple computers but is also available for Windows PCs. You may also give some thought to using a CRM that tracks fundraising activities. Exceed! Basic (http://www.telosa.com/software-non-profits), for example, is a software program resident on your PC that tracks donor updates and e-mail campaigns.

There are also CRMs that are not resident on your computer and exist instead as a subscription-based "cloud" Internet service. Bloomerang (https://bloomerang.com) and DonorPerfect (http://www.donorperfect.com) are two such product that focus on managing fundraising programs as well as tracking contacts. Each of these solutions charges by the month and the price scales up dramatically after the first 1,000 records.

From my perspective, I like idea of "owning" our own data outright, not being saddled with a subscription, and feel somewhat more secure having the data on our own computer's security system rather than trusting the cloud-based security of a vendor. Whichever option you choose, it's worth checking out TechSoup (in "Viva TechSoup!" later in this chapter) to see if discounted products are available.

COLLECTIONS DATABASE SOFTWARE

You'll also need database software if you have a collection of objects that you'll need to log as current or potential museum collections or archival materials. We use Microsoft Access for our film database, but we did have to set up fields and rules. We love it because we can customize fields specific to the films that comprise our collection. Access, however doesn't allow you to embed photos, something that PastPerfect (http://museumsoftware.com) does.

PastPerfect Museum Software is a terrific product that not only catalogues your collection but also has a CRM contact management system that lists donors, membership renewals, and volunteer hours. It also will allow you to upload photos and does many other useful tasks. At $695, this comprehensive product is a good one if you're eventually going to create a formal museum or archive. The issue we had with PastPerfect was that it wasn't optimized for film archives and we couldn't add the custom fields we needed. So before choosing PastPerfect, do ensure that it meets your needs. A good way to do this is to draw a chart of all the fields you'll need to log the objects in your collection, then talk to a PastPerfect representative to ensure that it will do the job.

FINANCIAL SOFTWARE

Whether you're keeping the books yourself or have a volunteer CFO, keeping the books electronically will make it easier to do reports, create profit and loss statements, and print it all out legibly for your corporate logbook. Intuit's QuickBooks Premier Edition (www.intuit.com) offers a Nonprofit edition that allows up to three users, so your

CFO, CEO, and another user can easily have access to current financial data.

PHOTO-PROCESSING SOFTWARE

It's expensive, but Adobe's Photoshop (www.adobe.com/products) is the king of the castle if you need to process photographs. It's been invaluable to us in allowing the conversion of photos that will look good on our website. We can adjust the resolution, add contrast and brightness, and cut the size and pixels so we're not bleeding bandwidth when we upload a photo. Basic features are simple to use out of the box, but its more powerful features require more time to acquire proficiency. Some time ago, I volunteered to assist a museum in Cuzco, Peru, that was engaged in transferring glass-plate negatives of turn-of-the century photographs to online positives. Photoshop allowed us to transfer the huge number of images quickly, with superior resolution and black-and-white balance. A ten-minute tutorial was needed, but even novices were proficient within a very short amount of time.

BACKUP SOFTWARE AND WEB-BASED BACKUP

If you're using a stand-alone PC system, you really do need to back up your file on a regular basis (if you're in the cloud, backup should be done by your provider, automatically and regularly). Many companies offer stand-alone backup products, but we've found Acronis True Image backup and recovery software (www.acronis.com) to be comprehensive and easy to use. We back our data up on one of two two-terabyte USB-connected hard drives that we alternately swap out every backup. We perform our backup every night, and an hour later it's done. You can get these drives for somewhere around $80 right now and the technology should continue to get less expensive for even more memory as time goes on.

You can also subscribe to a cloud-based backup utility instead of doing it yourself on a separate hard drive. Doing it via the cloud will be more expensive, with the advantage that it's automated and you won't have to remember to do it on an ongoing basis. There are caveats that you'll want to be aware of if you back up into the cloud. Some companies have a maximum data retention time frame. Other are not optimized for mobile devices, important if your organization does a lot of work on laptop computers. Companies that offer web-hosted backup include Acronis (www.acronis.com), BackBlaze (www.back blaze.com), Crashplan (www.crashplan.com), Druva (www.druva.com), and Mozy (www.mozy.com). About.com's Tim Fisher has written an article on the subject that's well worth reading, "39 Online Backup Services Reviewed" (http://pcsupport.about.com/od/maintenance/tp/online_backup_services.htm).

INTERNET SECURITY SOFTWARE

Pardon me for being puzzled, but I've talked to a lot of people recently who don't have Internet security software installed on computers that access the Internet on a regular basis. Some of these folks have been hacked and have had dangerous Trojans, worms, and bots installed by Internet crooks (I've done tech support for several of them). Please don't let this be you. We use Trend Micro (www.trendmicro.com) and like the fact that telephone tech support is always available. There are a number of others on the market, including Kaspersky, McAfee, and Symantec. Be sure you use a security solution.

A NOTE ABOUT MICROSOFT

When we began using Microsoft Office products, it was relatively easy to buy the suite (we use Word, Access, and the Excel spreadsheet) and affordable. Microsoft now encourages buyers to have a yearly subscription, and the stand-alone products only support one user. Microsoft continues to evolve its pricing plans, which, judging from its website (http://office.microsoft.com), only allow you to install on multiple computers if you buy by subscription. As a nonprofit, your least expensive way to acquire Microsoft products could very well be through TechSoup (see next section).

VIVA TECHSOUP! YOUR NONPROFIT DISCOUNTED SOFTWARE AND HARDWARE HEADQUARTERS

As a nonprofit organization, you'll have no better friend when you're acquiring software for your office than TechSoup (www.tech soup.org). As of this writing, more than fifty software producers are offering dramatically discounted products to nonprofits through Tech-Soup. Some of them are down-rev or remaindered, but they still do the job. Among these companies are Adobe, FileMaker, Intuit, Microsoft, and Symantec, all mentioned in this chapter. TechSoup also has a refurbished Computer Initiative Program that offers heavily discounted hardware. You must be a valid nonprofit and have an Employer Identification Number (EIN) from the IRS to join. You may also qualify as a library with an FSCS ID. It's that simple. You sign up, resister your organization, pick your product(s) and check eligibility status (some manufacturers limit the number of their products that you can buy via TechSoup in a given year). There are also rules for organization types and budgets. TechSoup is an essential resource for any sustainable nonprofit organization.

So now your office has been set up, and since you've already determined the technology you'll use to build your website, it's time to create it, launch it, and begin considering how you'll use social media to augment it.

Office Tools Checklist

Hardware

- Computer
- Printer and scanner
- USB backup hard drive

Software

- Word processor software
- OCR software
- Spreadsheet software
- CRM database
- Collections database software
- Financial software
- PDF software
- Photo-processing software
- Backup software
- Internet security software
- Register on www.techsoup.org

CHAPTER 5

Building and Maintaining Your Website, E-mail, Social Media and Business-Networking Presence

You need to have a good website and a functioning e-mail system. But you should also be looking into social media and business-networking options. A business-networking presence such as a LinkedIn profile is easy to build, and there's very little maintenance involved. If you're not yet comfortable or capable of working with social media such as Facebook and Twitter, I recommend that you find someone who is. The world of social media is changing the way many people interact, and it ripened along with the rise in economic importance of the Millennials, individuals born roughly between the years 1978 and 1992. They grew up in the Internet age and remain increasingly savvy about tools and techniques associated with electronic media. Keep these people in mind while you consider the value as well as the "how to" of social media. I'll revisit them later in this chapter.

The Importance of Your Website

Your website is the strongest element in your public "face," and your URL (Uniform Resource Locator, i.e., your web address) will have a prominent place on your business cards and any promotional material you may have. Your site doesn't have to be beautiful—a general rule in website construction is that beauty costs money—but it does have to be functional and informative. Functional means having good navigation and pages that don't go down or lead to nowhere. In terms of being informative, ensure that the builder(s) of your website has an ultimate goal of uploading to your site more information on your nonprofit's area of interest than is available anyplace else on the web. Sure, it's a lofty goal, but it's a good one, and you, your officers and volunteers should continually come up with ways to make it so. The more information you have, the more keywords will be picked up on search engines like Google, Yahoo, and Bing. Those keywords will drive increasing numbers of visitors to your site. If you want to make your website Really Beautiful, you can add videos, but that will increase the server space and bandwidth needed to support your website and that may end up costing you more money than a simple, informative web presence. Still pictures, when you keep each of them down to 100 kb or so, don't tend to use up lots of memory and bandwidth, but videos can. As an underfunded nonprofit, you'll want to keep your monthly expenses to a minimum. As I'll explain, paying a lot of money to host your website and paying someone every time you have to add content are two money sinks that you'll want to avoid. Initially, you'll need to buy a URL and select a web-hoisting provider. Following that, you'll need to design and build your site, uploading content as you go along. Let's get started.

Buying a URL and Selecting a Web-Hosting Provider

Your website doesn't have to be expensive to design, upload, or maintain. Maintenance can represent an ever and dramatically increasing cost if you're paying someone an hourly fee to do your uploading, and those fees may very well prevent you from wanting to add important content as you grow. And it's vitally important to continually add content and update your website. I mention this early on, as you should keep this in mind as you read further and choose how you want to build your site.

You can create and own a URL for just a few dollars per year from companies like VoxDomains, WhoIs, and Wix. These companies can also host your website. It isn't expensive to have a company host your website, either, providing you don't use a lot of server space and bandwidth. Server space represents the amount of memory your site takes up on your server (in your case, that will probably mean a remote server owned by your web-hosting provider). "Bandwidth" refers to the traffic between your web server and the Internet. And if you're going to require lots of server space and bandwidth, you can partner with other nonprofits that will pay for it, so you don't have to.

To make it a little clearer, here's how those two elements impact a nonprofit like ours. Here at the AFA, we have a sponsored film initiative that results in the digitization and uploading of films. People do want to see moving images, and bandwidth and server space costs preclude us from hosting viewable films on our own website. Instead of hosting those films on our site, therefore, we upload them to the Academic Film Archive of North America collection site at the Internet Archive (http://archive.org/details/academic_films), which hosts them free of charge and handles the bandwidth as well. We then link those films directly to topical text on our own website. Viewers can thus see the films by either going directly to our collection space on the Internet Archive or clicking on a link in one of our web pages and getting there indirectly (it's so fast, it's seamless). If your nonprofit has important material that requires expensive bandwidth and server space, find a partner or affiliate that will host for you and just link to the material from your own low-cost website. Bob Barcus (www.myapheus.com/how-much-server-space-and-bandwith-do-you-really-need) has a simple-to-understand explanation of server and bandwidth on his blog.

Acquiring Web Design Software or a Web-Based Design Platform

You start with web-development tools. Here at the AFA, none of us writes HTML code, which is the source for our website. Since we wanted to build the website ourselves, we needed to find a WYSIWYG (What You See Is What You Get) program that would allow for easy design, easy upload, and that we could maintain into the future without the need to pay a programmer or uploader. Our trick was to use an old program from Microsoft called FrontPage 2003. This program is marvelous, although no longer supported by Microsoft. No matter, because we've never needed support. Our 2003 version supports something called "navigation view," which allows us to build pages into the web by physically dragging and dropping pages right into the graphical representation of the site map (Microsoft's Expression Web, which replaced FrontPage, didn't have a navigation view last time we checked). To upload new content, we simply copy and paste from Microsoft Word right into these pages and we add photos by inserting them from our computer's picture files. That's how we do it, and it allows us to easily and consistently add new content without having to pay anyone to do it. As I mentioned earlier, we let the Internet Archive handle our moving images.

In addition, to software-based web-building tools, there are also a number of website-building solutions on the Internet. Three of these are VoxDomains (www.voxdomains.com), WhoIs (www.whois.com), and Wix.com (www.wix.com). As mentioned earlier, these companies offer hosting solutions and other options as well.

As I've emphasized, paying a website consultant to design and maintain your website can be expensive. And the more expensive it becomes, the less you may want to constantly add great material to it. In the radio business, engineers loved building arcane customized transmitters that only they could maintain, effectively giving them jobs for life. Don't let a similar situation befall your organization as it goes about creating a website. Many website-building products require someone who can do HTML coding, so rather than be dependent on someone who will require ongoing funding, I encourage you to find a volunteer who will be happy to build your website and teach you how to easily add content to it. Let him or her use the tool he or she is most familiar with. By learning how to update and add content yourself, you're guaranteeing sustainability if that person moves on. Today, thousands—if not millions—of teenagers and young adults, the Millennials I discussed earlier, are savvy enough to build terrific websites, so there's value in cultivating young volunteers to handle those tasks. They're also, as a rule, hooked into social media as well, and that's important, so you'll also want to consider those options.

Conceptualizing, building, and maintaining a website can at first seem daunting, but it's a valuable experience. I'll confess that here at the AFA we built ours on the fly and added things and tweaked it as time went by. What was important was that we didn't spend months agonizing over the initial design. We ran the tutorial in our web software and added our own content to it. We liked it so much that we immediately published it. It wasn't glamorous, but it was functional, and we wanted web crawlers to note our presence (see below). You can rapid-prototype, as we did, and get it up right away or take a more formal design approach, which will take longer. If the latter appeals to you, TechSoup's Chris Peters has written a post based on the traditional "Waterfall" method of software design (Analysis, Design, Develop, Test, Maintenance) that, while time-consuming, will go a long way to debugging your web concept before it launches (http://www.techsoup. org/support/articles-and-how-tos/tips-for-designing-or-redesigning-a-nonprofit-website).

Building Remarkable Content

Coming up with entertaining, informative, and important content for your website is an ongoing project, but it needn't be difficult. You'll begin by designing your home page, which ideally contains your mission statement, defines whom you serve, and how you serve them. You should create a table of contents that will become your directory, which is most often found at the top or at either side of all pages. "Who We Are" and "Contact Us" are two important tabs or directory clicks that allow you to give brief bios, pictures, and contact information. Whether you're a start-up nonprofit or a mature one, you should always be looking for informative and interesting content to put on your website. How do you find it?

You have a passion for the area of your organization's expertise, and you or your colleagues have probably written articles, essays, or even white papers on the subject. If you've also discovered great content written by others, you can secure permission from them, then upload them to a "Resources" page. Often, they'll let you use the content in return for a link to their own sites. You also can develop a "Links" page, and link to a number of other sites that provide information that relates to your subject area. Here at the AFA, we started building biographies and filmographies of filmmakers whose work we thought was important. We found it amazing that most of them hadn't compiled either of these documents, so in doing so we provided an important resource for scholars, media historians, and the filmmakers themselves. So that became a directory for a "Filmmakers Bios" page and we cascaded those biographies alphabetically from that page. Many filmmakers had interviews that had been conducted with them during the course of their careers and were in paper format. They mailed the interviews to us and we scanned them and attached them as separate, linked pages on the website. That's one way we were able to get informative content at no cost.

It's important to thank your donors, so do put up a "donors" page. And if you do have a special sponsorship project, like our Save A Film initiative, that deserves a special page, too (see "Checklist" at the end of this chapter for a sample initial website directory).

A Free Search Utility for Your Website

As your website grows, you'll want to build a site map, which is a single page that offers links to all your web pages (for an example, visit http://www.afana.org/sitemap.htm). Site maps are routinely visited by major search engines and make it easier for viewers to navigate your site when they're looking for something specific. You'll also want to embed a search field on your home page so visitors can search on various keywords within your site. The best free site search application we've found is FreeFind (www.freefind.com), which offers two versions. The free version includes ads, which we find nonintrusive. The paid version offers site search ad-free.

Place a "Donation" Button on Your Website

It's relatively easy to place a "Donation" button on your website. You can place it on your home page, your Donations page, or both.

PayPal, for example, has a utility for nonprofits that allows people to donate to a nonprofit by accepting donations made with credit cards, debit cards, and PayPal, with no monthly, setup, or cancellation fees, and offers transaction fees that are lower than for for-profit entities. Through its nonprofit page (https://www.paypal.com/us/cgi-bin/?cmd=_donate-intro-outside) PayPal provides simple-to-load HTML code, which you can copy and paste to your preferred web page. It's quick, and it took us here at the AFA, with no coding experience, fewer than ten minutes to sign up, copy the code, transfer it to our web page, and upload it to our website. Google offers a similar capability geared toward nonprofit organizations at http://checkout.google.com/seller/npo.

Keywords and SEO (Search Engine Optimization)

Keywords are identifiers that search engines use, through web crawlers, to index your website, so as you create web content, keep in mind that utilizing synonyms can have real value. If you have that ichigenkin website, you'll therefore want to identify that instrument in as many ways as you can. For instance "one-string ichigenkin," "one-stringed ichigenkin," and "Japanese ichigenkin" are all identifiers you would want to use. Use your imagination and brainstorm with your team, as there are many more. Basically you're trying to increase the odds that anyone searching for broad information germane to your topic area, as well as information particular to your organization's area of expertise, will arrive at your site. A little more complex is the concept of search engine optimization (SEO), which is more about the *science* of choosing words and phrases that will be more attractive to search engines. This involves not only keywords but also how you name your pages, taking into consideration how often certain words are searched for and their comparative rarity in consideration with other websites that are using the same or similar words. There are two very good resources on the web that explain the SEO and web-crawling process nicely. Visit Google's post (https://support.google.com/webmasters/answer/35291?hl=en) and Moz.com's Beginner's Guide to SEO (http://

moz.com/beginners-guide-to-seo). In addition, there are SEO-based content management and hosting companies like HubSpot that make it relatively easy to figure it all out (www.hubspot.com), although adopting its technology involves both initial startup and monthly fees.

You may also want to give some thought to web analytics, so you can better track what's happening on your website in terms of visitor behavior. Google actively encourages nonprofits to use its free analytics tools and even offers a free online Analytics Academy https://support.google.com/analytics/answer/4553001?hl=en&ref_topic=3424286). Connecting Up also has an easy-to-understand overview of analytics in general (www.connectingup.org/learn/articles/introduction-google-analytics).

E-mail Versus Direct Mail

Your website should be the foundation of your public presence, but it's still, essentially, a "pull" medium, in which people have to come to you. Therefore, having an e-mail list is critical, and there are at least a couple of good ways to go about doing it. Mozilla is a free software community that produces the Firefox web browser and the Thunderbird e-mail application (http://www.mozilla.org/en-US/thunderbird). We've found Thunderbird to be pretty much bulletproof, and it hasn't suffered a glitch in more than a decade of use. One of the reasons we like it is we feel more secure having our e-mail files resident on our own computer, rather than having them live "in the cloud" on the Internet. If you don't want to host your e-mail system on your own computer, companies such as Google, Microsoft, and Yahoo provide no-fee options.

Another option is that you may be able to integrate e-mail with your CRM (Customer Relationship Management) program. E-mail is an important "push" technology that is critical for getting the word out to your nonprofit's audience, so start collecting e-mail addresses from your friends and supporters if you haven't yet done so. I strongly recommend periodically (at least once a quarter) publishing an e-mail-based newsletter that contains news as well as updates on your programs and events. Always make a brief mention of how people can make donations, but don't flog it *ad nauseum*, as your e-mail may go into the spam folder if you do. For more ideas on building compelling e-mail newsletters, see the chapter "Publicity and Publishing: Getting Others to Know About Your Work" later in this book.

I don't care very much for sending direct postal mail, especially from rented lists, and I don't think you as an underfunded nonprofit should, either. Printing and mailing costs are not worth absorbing and e-mail is more pervasive (again, see the chapter "Publicity and Publishing: Getting Others to Know About Your Work" for some additional tips on crafting good e-mails).

One last very important item regarding e-mail: You don't want to be perceived as a spammer. Particularly in the case of an event you're promoting, please don't send out more than one e-mail per week. Many people unsubscribe to lists because they feel they're being harassed and are beset by donor fatigue. Your home-grown e-mail list is important, so please don't harm its effectiveness through an endless storm of e-mails that could cause valuable people to exit the list. In terms of general e-mail etiquette, it's also a good idea to have a rider at the bottom of your e-mail advising people how to unsubscribe if they wish.

Business Networking, Social Media, and Blogs

In addition, you'll want to become engaged with the business networking site LinkedIn. It's worth looking into social media options, such as Facebook, as well. These technologies continue to evolve, and I encourage you to identify a volunteer or officer to tap into his or her social media expertise as you look to evolve a public identity. The "cutting-edge" face of nonprofits has moved into the arena of business-networking media as well. These days, I think it's necessary to have a profile under LinkedIn (www.linkedin.com). LinkedIn represents a business network, not a social network. It's free, and you can set up a personal profile and biography connected with your nonprofit. Best of all, it's not time-consuming to maintain. As soon as you sign up, begin by sending invitations to people you know at other affiliate organizations and nonprofits. As a matter of etiquette, I suggest you only invite people with whom you've either talked to personally or carried on an e-mail discussion. Make it a point to continue adding these people to your contact list. After several weeks, you'll start discovering that people with whom you're speaking for the first time will know people you know, and you can make reference to that as you communicate with them. That's the power of LinkedIn.

Social media providers, such as Facebook and Twitter, can also be important to your public profile, but our experience is that they, unlike LinkedIn, can be time-consuming unless one of your volunteers takes on the task of contributing material and/or maintaining them. Facebook encourages two-way communication, while Twitter essentially allows you to post short messages. WordPress (http://wordpress.org) is a blog application that can sit on your website, allowing you to instantly publish posts to which others can subscribe, via RSS (Rich Site Summary, also known as Really Simple Syndication) feeds. If you're not sure just where to begin with social media, Frank Barry of Blackbaud has written a very good ten-page white paper that provides excellent background on the concept and gives you some things you can do yourself to get started as well (https://www.blackbaud.com/files/resources/downloads/WhitePaper_BBIS_SocialMediaStrategy.pdf).

There is a growing body of research that suggests social media are constantly in a state of flux and what is popular today will be passé tomorrow. Lisa Goddard, Online Marketing Director of the Capital Area Food Bank, as interviewed by Neff and Moss, mentions that Facebook use is decreasing among young adults and teens, that mobile use is increasing with this group, and that "any digital marketing strategy I implement must be flexible enough so I don't have to start from scratch every time a hot new social media tool is on the scene."[1]

It might be of value to find a volunteer in the Millennial generation who is willing to build a Facebook page for your organization and manage it. In addition to enhancing your public profile, there are potential affiliates and other interesting communities that don't have a website but do have a Facebook page. One such group is the Hortisexuals (https://www.facebook.com/pages/Hortisexuals/263053410382452), a horticultural community that hosts tours to botanical and private gardens (yes, they've been to Borneo to see the Rafflesia).[2]

I emphatically believe in making things easy, because when they're easy they tend to get done on time and done well. You do need a website and e-mail, and I'd recommend that you be as hands-on as possible in those two critically important areas. Again, if you're not an expert in social media and don't aspire to be one, your best choice for engaging in social media like Facebook, Twitter, and WordPress is to identify a volunteer well versed in these technologies and gain agreement that he or she will set them up and maintain them for you. And I do want to reemphasize the importance of signing up for and using LinkedIn.

A Cautionary Note Regarding Web-Based Meetings

Social media now makes it relatively easy to set up online meetings. The advantage is that people don't have to transport themselves to a central meeting place. The disadvantage can be that people start arranging online meetings all the time, for everything under the sun. I'm on several committees at one nonprofit organization to which I belong, which holds a conference every year. Several years ago, each committee began hosting online meetings throughout the year, and seemingly not a week goes by that I do not receive several e-mails regarding an online meeting that's being set up. I already have too many usernames and passwords to remember, and I long for the day that committee business could be taken care of during the annual meeting, with a few follow-up e-mails throughout the year as we all worked independently. Earlier, I mentioned meeting fatigue as a factor to consider when cobbling together a board of directors. But meeting fatigue also includes having too many meetings. Just because social media makes it easier to have meetings doesn't mean you have to add more to your officers' and volunteers' schedules.

Volunteers are your most important asset, and you don't want to burn them out. To build and maintain a website, administrate e-mail, and engage in business networking and social media, you'll need to involve your volunteers. They are the subject of the next chapter.

Checklist

- Buy a URL.
- Identify a web-hosting provider.
- Identify a volunteer web developer who will build and maintain your site.
- Acquire web design software or a web-based design platform.
- Identify sources for informative web content and contact them.
- Load your website with content that contains keywords particular to your organization's area of expertise.
- Acquire a search utility for your website.
- Place a "donation" button on your website.
- Develop a LinkedIn profile.
- Find a volunteer conversant with social media and blogging and adopt those technologies.

Sample Webpage Directory

Index
Who We Are
Donations
Sponsor a Project
Resources
Links
Site Map
Contact Us

CHAPTER 6

Volunteers: Your
Most Valuable Asset

As mentioned in the earlier "Don't Quit Your Day Job" chapter, I recommend that you begin as a 100 percent volunteer organization. That includes you, as the founder and director. Perhaps it's a moot point; if you're a start-up or a small nonprofit with very little money, you probably won't be tempted with hiring employees anyway.

But no mistake about it, your volunteer organization can be exceptional if it adopts, as authors Alison Green and Jerry Hauser suggest, a "culture of excellence."[1] I believe that high performance and an insistence on quality are the hallmarks of a successful, sustainable operation. The principles as defined by Green and Hauser are "relentlessness," "a high bar for performance," "scrutiny of ideas," "accountability," "transparency and commitment to continuous improvement," and "mission integrity." These are self-defining, and encompass everything in your day-to-day operations, from minutiae such as grammar and spelling in all public communications to the manner in which meetings are conducted and how and when projects are completed.

Being all-volunteer or heavily laden with volunteers is to your advantage. With each employee, your organization is responsible for a plethora of laws relating to employment, termination, and taxes. You'll also need to look at insurance. There is an ever-growing body of law surrounding job discrimination against protected classes, which might include sexual orientation, age, gender, religion, and ethnicity. You could be sued, too, for any one of a number of different employment-related reasons, spurious or not. As Green and Hauser suggest, if any potential evidence of discrimination exists, call a lawyer first before taking any action.[2]

As a guerrilla nonprofit, you will indeed be thinking radically and unconventionally if you determine that the time is not right—or perhaps will never be right—to hire employees. If you're a director, I'll bet you want to be more focused on your mission than on personnel issues. But if you have employees, you pro forma own the responsibility, regardless of whether you have a Human Resources person or not.

Here's one example of a personnel issue that underscores the value of keeping your nonprofit as 100 percent volunteer as possible. We had a challenging situation with a volunteer who had a number of responsibilities. We had painstakingly cobbled together a group of students from a university that had agreed to do a complete inventory of a significant film donation located at an off-site facility. The volunteer in question had the only set of keys and made arrangements to meet the inventory team. Our volunteer didn't show up at the agreed-upon time and didn't return any phone calls, either, including mine. This was a professionally embarrassing situation for us and didn't inspire a lot of confidence in us from the student inventory team, either. So we unilaterally terminated the volunteer relationship with the individual, changed the locks, and managed to get the inventory done on another day. As management consultant Peter Drucker said, when writing about people working in your organization, "If they try, they deserve another chance. If they don't try, make *sure* they leave."[3] This uncomfortable situation was made easier by the fact that this person was a volunteer, so all parties just "walked away" and went on with their lives. It might not have been this easy had the volunteer instead been an employee.

Yet another reason to stay "lean and mean" on the employee issue is the possibility of running into debt. One book on nonprofits suggests the possibility of borrowing money during tough times, recommending borrowing from board members and banks and extending credit card limits. I recommend instead that you control your finances to the extent that you never borrow money. Why should a board member or bank extend credit to an organization that is wrestling with trying to stay afloat?

A Note About Liabilities

If you read all the literature regarding the multiple forms of insurance "needed" to run a nonprofit, you might very well end up thinking that forming a nonprofit just isn't worth it. Standard Liability, D&O (directors and officers), and volunteers insurance are just three, to start off with. As I've already noted, not having any employees at all means that you're not burdened with insurance related to having employees.

We've managed to get by without insurance because we run a pretty tight ship. Our volunteers don't engage in strenuous physical activity. They don't drive people around on archive-related business. We make it a rule that no minor volunteers engage in any activity with us without at least one of their parents present and in view at all times. We don't want our organization exposed to potential abuse issues and can't run a background check on all volunteers. We've had very few non-adult volunteers, but when we do, having a parent right there is an absolute.

We believe in running an organization that is fair to everyone, treats all with respect, and has a "do unto others" philosophy. No matter how good you try to be, we are living in a litigious society. You're starting or operating your organization with little or no money, so strongly consider doing everything in such a way that you'll never have to hire legal representation. Even though you may be in the right, the costs associated with adjudicating anything will guarantee that you'll lose, financially.

One real advantage of having a 501(c)(3) is that it limits the liability of individuals operating in the name of the nonprofit, including unpaid debts and unsatisfied lawsuits. A creditor may expect relief from the nonprofit corporation but cannot pursue the personal assets of officers, employees, or volunteers. In terms of volunteers, they're generally protected when they work within their assigned tasks, perform them in a reasonable manner, and don't commit crimes when volunteering. Much of this has been covered under the Volunteer Protection Act of 1997, established by Congress as a protection for volunteers for any injuries incurred or damages they might cause when engaged in the normal scope of volunteer activities (the text of the law can be read at http://

www.gpo.gov/fdsys/pkg/PLAW-105publ19/pdf/PLAW-105publ19.pdf).
Of special note are several elements listed in section 4:

SEC. 4. LIMITATION ON LIABILITY FOR VOLUNTEERS.

(a) LIABILITY PROTECTION FOR VOLUNTEERS.—Except as provided in subsections (b) and (d), no volunteer of a nonprofit organization or governmental entity shall be liable for harm caused by an act or omission of the volunteer on behalf of the organization or entity if—

(1) the volunteer was acting within the scope of the volunteer's responsibilities in the nonprofit organization or governmental entity at the time of the act or omission;

(2) if appropriate or required, the volunteer was properly licensed, certified, or authorized by the appropriate authorities for the activities or practice in the State in which the harm occurred, where the activities were or practice was undertaken within the scope of the volunteer's responsibilities in the nonprofit organization or governmental entity;

(3) the harm was not caused by willful or criminal misconduct, gross negligence, reckless misconduct, or a conscious, flagrant indifference to the rights or safety of the individual harmed by the volunteer; and

(4) the harm was not caused by the volunteer operating a motor vehicle, vessel, aircraft, or other vehicle for which the State requires the operator or the owner of the vehicle, craft, or vessel to—

(A) possess an operator's license; or

(B) maintain insurance.

It should be noted that the VPA itself doesn't covers volunteers' personal property losses in case of theft. It may, therefore, be advisable to let your volunteers know that any potential theft losses of their own property would have to be covered under the terms of their own renter's or homeowner's policies.

Nonprofits have been known to have been victimized by employee theft that occurred when people with financial responsibility absconded with funds. I've known Michael Selic, our CFO, for more than thirty years. I met him when he was the CEO for another nonprofit and I trust him. Unless you have that kind of relationship with the individual doing your accounting, do get references and perform an Internet search on him or her. You may also want to set your finances up so that two signatures must appear on every check, the director's and the CFO's.

A book I read recently discussed drug testing as a criterion for volunteering. Personally, I don't care what people eat, drink, smoke, or ingest when they're not working with us. If your organization's mission doesn't include professional responsibilities for other humans (driving a bus, for example), I think it sets a good policy of trust in not being too concerned about what your volunteers do with their private lives.

Each state has its own liability laws in regard to charitable organizations. The Nonprofit Risk Management Center provides a free booklet describing these, available at http://www.nonprofitrisk.org/downloads/state-liability.pdf, broken down by state and with references to case law and specific codes.

There can always be gray areas in terms of what constitutes liability, so consulting an attorney (a good reason to have one on your Board of Officers) may be warranted and recommended if the activities of your volunteers aren't entirely within the scope of their duties as indicated by the Volunteer Protection Act.

Putting everything in perspective, as your nonprofit organization prospers you will find that there will be little as important to you as your volunteers. They'll share your passion and do a lot of the hard work, performing important simple and complex tasks that nobody really wants to do but have to be done if your organization is to succeed in its objectives. They will inspire you to keep the mission strong and directed and will raise your spirits on bad days when you've got your dauber down. They'll recruit other volunteers and think up a thousand good ideas you might not have come up with on your own. How do you find and choose them?

Finding and Choosing Your Volunteers

One of the most important elements to choosing your volunteers is to set expectations on both sides. You're looking for volunteers who will derive tremendous amounts of satisfaction in sharing a passion and making themselves feel worthwhile while affecting a positive change, societally, artistically, and personally. As your nonprofit is a small organization, you'll have to be honest with them, advising potential volunteers that there may not be a lot of limelight or public recognition involved. I've told our own volunteers that the significant contributions they're making to our mission as it relates to the preservation of important films may not be fully appreciated for years, perhaps decades, to come. But it will be valued, no mistake about it, in the future. You'll want your volunteers to share a vision, therefore, that extends into the future, rather than temporally, into next week or month.

Finding volunteers may require some outreach on your part. The "Publicity and Publishing: Getting Others to Know About Your Work" chapter provides a number of ways you can touch your local public. Telling the world that you're looking for volunteers is valuable way to potentially connect with them. Most of our volunteers originally attended our shows and became regulars. Some of them were young people who were fascinated with archaic technology (16mm film projectors). Stephanie Studebaker, a college student, borrowed a projector, took a brief tutorial, brought it home, and got her family and friends involved as well. That represented six volunteers getting together, having a good time, watching films, and documenting them. They're among the best volunteers we ever had. These folks fall into the Millennials category I discuss in the "Building and Maintaining Your Website, E-mail, Social Media and Business Networking Presence" chapter. In their book, Beth Kantner and Allison H. Fine[4] describe how volunteers in this age group tend to be project focused and commonly move on to other interests once the project is finished. This stands to reason, as their college situations, jobs, physical locations, and passions are continually changing. We always welcome them, for their project commitment, energy, drive, and ethical perspective.

What's particularly interesting about Millennial volunteers is how similar they are to the Baby Boomers during the Vietnam era. Neil Blumenthal, CEO of Warby Parker eyewear and a Millennial himself, noted a few tips recently about working with Millennials. As quoted in *Inc.* magazine, he eschews the idea that they're "entitled" and mentions that they work well in an environment with a strong mission statement that embraces social values, while needing to understand how their work translates into the "big picture."[5] Sounds exactly like their Baby Boomer and Generation X (born 1966–1976) predecessors when those groups were below thirty years of age. The Millennials, too, will be in a few years (or already are) managing the next generation. In essence, today's

6. *Volunteers: Your Most Valuable Asset*

Millennials are just like Boomers were at that age. So if you're a little bit older and managing Millennial volunteers, my recommendation is that you try to remember what you were like and what motivated you when you were that age. If you do, I think you'll agree with Blumenthal that they're terrific workers.

When looking for exceptional volunteers of all ages, don't ignore local employee volunteer programs sponsored by companies operating in your community. Increasingly, companies are embracing the idea of engaging their employees in the nonprofit world. NetApp and Google are two such companies that aggressively promote volunteerism. NetApp's Volunteer Time Off (VTO) program (http://www.netapp.com/us/careers/life/giving-back.aspx) enables each employee to volunteer up to five consecutive days per year, with full pay, during regular business hours to support the nonprofit organizations or schools of their choice. In calendar year 2012, 2,942 NetApp employees around the world donated 49,058 hours of volunteer time during business hours valued at $2,725,607. NetApp allows employees to bring nonprofits of their choice in to make company presentations at brown-bag lunches. Although corporate headquarters is in the Silicon Valley, it promotes volunteerism in its offices globally. Yet another company, Google, encourages its employees to donate a day each June to community service projects. In 2013, its employees logged more than 50,000 hours of volunteer time (https://www.google.com/giving/index.html).

Always be looking for project-specific volunteers possessing talents that none of your core volunteers have. One of our most memorable film reviewers was Daniel Comarazamy, a math major at San José State, who attended our shows and offered to volunteer. We had just gotten a hundred or so math films that none of us wanted to watch but were important for our film archive (our core volunteers are liberal arts and engineering folks but no true math whizzes). Daniel borrowed a film projector, watched all of those math films, did terrific reviews, and even wrote out the formulas discussed in the films, which we placed in the film cans. That's performance!

So how do your core volunteers (who, after all, are your potential officers) become engaged? Core volunteers do a lot of things. When we began doing our public, free-of-charge film shows back in the early days, our core volunteers set up tables and chairs, lit table candles, then put everything away when the program was over. They loved the films, wanted to be part of the experience, and quickly learned the intricacies of running film projectors. Soon, they designed their own programs and hosted the shows entirely on their own. They were an important element to our success.

Don't be surprised if your core volunteers go to great lengths to help ensure the success of your organization. As media libraries all over the country found out about us, they began offering significant film donations that we wanted to take, even though we didn't always have rack space for them. Our core volunteers gave us their basements for temporary film storage while we figured out just where we were going to put all that material. They got their neighbors to do it, too. One result of this effort was that the volunteers began watching and reviewing films on their own, allowing us to enter data into our collection database faster and more efficiently. You may find, as we did, that your core volunteers can turn an emergency into an asset.

Staging Larger Volunteer Projects

Core volunteers will spread the word and get others involved as project-specific volunteers, too. The projects resulting from these relationships can have significant impact on your underfunded organization. This can be extremely valuable, for example, in terms of facilities challenges, particularly when you're not paying rent and your benefactor doesn't have the means to improve your space. We at the AFA have a wonderful example of how such a project can make a difference. For years, we'd been plagued with donated shelving at our archive venue that had been installed incorrectly and therefore sagged dangerously under the weight of heavy film cans. We're in earthquake country, and none of us wanted to be anywhere near those shelves when the next temblor hit. One of our core volunteers had a friend whose son needed to perform an Eagle Scout project for a nonprofit like ours. They all had a discussion about our situation, and Thomas Peterson's project ended up being a complete disassembly and retrofit of those shelves. That project included taking more than 5,000 films out of the shelves, tagging and classifying them in their new bins, and putting the information in spreadsheets so we could, for the first time, easily locate films. Thomas crafted a professional proposal and had it accepted by his Eagle Scout management team. He got other scouts, friends and family involved. They found a resource for all the new parts (the old manufacturer had gone out of business), drove 350 miles to Los Angeles to pick everything up, and painted everything so that it would all match. Over the course of a month, he managed the whole project and got everything done. This was a vitally important project. Not only were the films and shelves secured, but we could now instantly locate any film, instead of having to manually search through thousands of film cans, also. Our total cash outlay consisted of five pizzas and a few soft drinks.

Since we're talking about the Scouts, I think it's worth having a brief discussion about the big political world out there and how it might—or might not—impact volunteer projects such as the one I just described. The Boy Scouts of America had been in the news a lot during the time we agreed to have Thomas and team come in and help us. As I mentioned earlier, the news was about their policy concerning the involvement of gay people in their organization. It was a national policy with which we disagreed. Our organization embraces diversity. Our choice was to not engage in a discussion about gay rights in the course of working with this San Francisco Bay Area Eagle Scout group. While we certainly have our opinions, they had nothing to do with the matter at hand, and we welcomed the volunteers.

You will have volunteers coming from a number of different philosophical perspectives. Some of our volunteers are religious people, but some are not. Here we all share the philosophy of how important it is to complete our mission by saving films from destruction and providing public access, so we concentrate on what we have in common, rather than on elements of our personal lives and thoughts that aren't particularly relevant to our nonprofit's goals and objectives.

Your successful nonprofit will evolve as you develop new ideas and projects, and some of the best ideas will come from your volunteers. Most important, they'll usually make suggestions by saying, "Here's a great idea; here's how *we* can do it," rather than "Here's a really great idea; here's how *you* can do it."

If you're a Type A individual, you may be used to doing everything yourself, and you may want it to remain that way. I'm hoping the examples I've given will change your mind. If you can't think of a way to get volunteers involved, here's one. Your passion and mission may be worth a book, and at the very least, you can self-publish it as an eBook or on a print-on-demand platform. You can make it a nonprofit venture. If you do, why not engage others in photos, layout, and text? That will give you an opportunity to thank them in print, too (read more about the value of authoring a book in the "Publicity and Publishing: Getting Others to Know About Your Work" chapter).

Think outside the box a bit as you look for volunteers. People who are working as consultants or have jobs with flexible schedules are valuable. So are stay-at-home parents who have a few hours on many days while their children are at school. Many of these parents have office skills and are savvy when it comes to word processing, spreadsheets, databases, and financial software. They can lower your equipment costs by using their own computer systems until you get a system donated to your nonprofit.

I don't expect our volunteers to be perfect, only that they want to be here and believe in our vision. Sometimes they just want to hang out, and that's fine, too. It's important to create a good vibe, and even people hanging around will generally do something of value when asked. I was fortunate enough to have volunteered at KTAO-FM, a noncommercial radio station in Los Gatos, California, run by Lorenzo Milam in the early 1970s.[6] Lorenzo had a remarkably laissez-faire attitude in terms of what his on-air volunteer staff could do. His only rules, really, were to create unique programming, be unafraid to experiment, and not put the FCC license at risk. Decades later, a station reunion was held and it was remarkable to hear how many people remembered so much of what occurred, and so fondly. I'd like you to view the experience that your volunteers have with you, and will have with you, in a similar fashion. Another measure of success to which you'll want to aspire may actually occur in the future. What will your volunteers say about you, and their experience with you and the organization, in a few decades?

I've got six simple basic rules for working with volunteers:

6. Volunteers: Your Most Valuable Asset

1. Make sure they know what they're doing is important and how it will contribute to the future.

2. Ensure that they know how to accomplish the task at hand, give them some mentoring, and provide a deadline for when it needs to be finished.

3. Follow up occasionally to see how they're doing and give them compliments.

4. Make sure they have fun.

5. Thank them constantly.

6. When they quit or move on, thank them again one last time and tell them how much they contributed, how much it was appreciated, and how they made a difference in terms of the future.

The "fun factor" is extremely important, and we try to build it in to every endeavor. For instance, we rely on volunteers to watch and document films. But we don't ask them to view films on subject areas in which they have no interest. We ask them to select films based on titles. Our volunteers therefore view films that they'll want to see and often invite friends over and make a night of it.

I encourage you to track your volunteers' hours, as occasionally a granting organization will request to see volunteer statistics in order to gauge the level of volunteerism in your operation. You may also need this information if you go through a formal audit procedure. A simple way is to give them a photocopied sheet with days of the week listed, which they can fill out and return to you every couple of weeks. You can also encourage your volunteers to track their hours online. Our-Volts (www.ourvolts.com), and YourVolunteers (www.yourvolunteers.com), for example, offer both free and subscription plans.

Whatever you do, please reconsider if you're considering asking your volunteers to sign a contract of any kind. Working with your organization is supposed to be fun and rewarding. It's not worth risking losing a great volunteer because he or she refused to sign your contract. And as I mention in the "Fund-Raising Programs and Techniques That Could Present Problems" chapter, I'd be very wary of asking them to engage in a telemarketing campaign that will subject them to rejection and abuse.

Avoiding Micromanaging

Author Peri H. Pakroo, J.D.,[7] has a terrific perspective on what she calls "founderitis," referring to the founder of a nonprofit who just can't keep his or her hands out of every pie. That would apply to an organization with a sole director, too. She recommends three things for everyone who occupies this type of management role:

1. Educate yourself on your proper role.
2. Let others do their jobs without interference.
3. Embrace situations in which you aren't the boss.

Items 2 and 3 are especially important. In the shelving project mentioned earlier, I was just another volunteer, reporting to our Eagle Scout project manager. I didn't even set the schedule for completion. I simply let everyone know that I was a resource when they needed me for anything, which was chiefly answering questions about various films and helping to haul films to their new shelf locations.

Letting others do their jobs without interference doesn't mean that you shouldn't offer yourself as a resource when needed. One of the best I've seen at delegating, letting go, checking in occasionally, and having an open door as a resource was Richard, a veteran director of sales teams at high-tech companies such as Cisco Systems, among others (he asked that his full name not be used). The people who reported to him all had sales quotas, so they were well aware of their objectives. Richard would meet with everyone weekly to check in and see how they were progressing. If it wasn't going well, he would ask an individual how he could best be a resource for him or her to achieve success. It was a great approach, as it avoided micromanaging and instead allowed Richard to offer himself as a resource to help everyone succeed. Some needed help more than others, and because Richard hired them he was committed to seeing them succeed. He added another note: "When they were successful for a month or two, I stopped checking in weekly, although I monitored the numbers. I wanted to step back because I didn't want to stifle their creativity, and wanted them to find new ways on their own of doing the job better." Every nonprofit with volunteers or employees should consider taking Richard's approach as an alternative to managing people heavy-handedly.

As a resource for your volunteers, I advocate that you act in a "teaching," rather than "telling" mode. When correcting a behavior or situation, consider using language that reinforces that principle. Rather than telling someone, "Here's what you did wrong," you might instead first tell the individual what he or she did well and then follow it up with, "And here's how you can make what you did even more powerful." There's a lot of value in keeping things positive, because it's more enjoyable for people to work with you when you take that approach. It's better to have them want to do something than "making" them do it. A technique advocated by Silicon Valley Creates' Audrey Wong is to use a "buddy system" when possible, pairing a more experienced volunteer with a newer one, thus facilitating the transfer of knowledge.[8]

As discussed earlier, Richard was essentially practicing what Alison Green and Jerry Hauser preach on the topic of delegation in their book *Managing to Change the World*.[9] They suggest three steps: "Agree on Expectations," "Stay Engaged," and "Create Accountability and Learning." That third step posits that the individual is responsible for results, both favorable and unfavorable. In either case, these factors represent learning opportunities that can be applied to future tasks and programs. In terms of agreeing on expectations, Green and Hauser suggest asking the individual to "repeat back" to you what he or she understands the task encompasses. For more detailed and complicated assignments, they suggest asking the individual to send the delegator an e-mail, outlining his or her understanding of the assignment.[10]

My "Sponsorships: Building a Definitive, Self-Sustaining, Permanent and Exciting Keynote Program" chapter offers still more ideas on how you can step out of the way while encouraging your volunteers to take the initiative and build something they create and manage themselves.

Choosing Your Board of Officers

You will have core volunteers who are with you continually and you will have project-specific volunteers, who take on significant initiatives. Important core volunteers would include your officers. You'll legally need to designate a Vice President as well as a CFO (or Treasurer), who'll keep your books straight, give a financial report at your yearly meeting, and file your tax return. You'll want to appoint a Secretary, who will keep the minutes of your meetings and ensure that they get inserted into your corporate logbook. I believe in choosing your officers from your volunteers. They know and love your organization, believe in its mission, and will be there in both good and challenging times.

The importance of the role of CFO/Treasurer cannot be overstated. I'd recommend finding someone who has a working knowledge of accounting software such as Intuit's QuickBooks (see the "Setting Up Your Sustainable Nonprofit Office" chapter). It's a good idea to identify someone to be your CFO as soon as you can, as IRS Form 1023 requires you to include financial information from the previous three years and you may need your CFO's assistance to sort and compile your data (see Chapter 3, "The First Step: Forming Your Nonprofit Corporation," for more on Form 1923). It's important to stay legal and your CFO should be constantly adding categorized income and expenses to your books. Make this an ongoing process so these data don't have to be entered at the last minute, at the end of your tax year. That way, he or she simply compiles the data, computes taxes (if any), files your tax return, and provides the year's financial reports for your corporate record book. To reiterate, don't let receipts pile up. Get them to your CFO on a timely basis so you can stay current.

In an ideal world, your Board of Officers would reflect the diversity in your community. This doesn't mean that you collect officers solely because they represent different genders, ethnicities, ages, and sexual preferences. But if your board is homogeneous, chances are you won't be attracting as many sponsors and donors as you'd like. People from different backgrounds will have a plethora of ideas you'd never have imagined and have venues for those ideas that you might not have considered. Enjoyment of the subject matter of your nonprofit isn't specific to gender, ethnicity, age, or sexual identity, either, and you'll want to be inclusive rather than exclusive. Building a diverse board will open your nonprofit to new opportunities and help pave the way to ongoing successes and acquiring new volunteers and donors.

There are differing philosophies within the nonprofit community on the criteria for putting people on the board. In many organizations the prime criterion is how much money the board member can raise.

Each board member is expected to "give-or-get" a fixed amount or lose his or her seat on the board (known popularly as "give, get, or get off"). Our philosophy here at the AFA is that we want our board folks to be great volunteers, helping to do the things that need to be done. Yes, they've come up with some wonderful ideas on raising money, and we've implemented them. But fund-raising has never been a requirement of our board. Here's a good test for you. Let's say you make raising a certain amount of money a requirement for being on your board. Your board officer fails to do it but is a fantastic volunteer who makes great contributions in meetings. Do you really want to kick that person off your board, thereby sending a message about values that you probably don't want to send?

Here's a pertinent story that emphasizes my point. One organization with whom we're familiar charges a $40,000 "give-or-get" fee to sit on the board. One capable and loved director did her bit every year and one year brought in $100,000 in an event she put together. Several years later, her domestic situation changed. She was a single parent and, even though an active board member, couldn't come up with the fee one year. She had to resign from the board she loved, and because they couldn't make exceptions the board accepted her resignation. She soon joined the board of another nonprofit that didn't have the financial stipulation. She missed serving on her old board, they missed her, but it was a fait accompli. Years of service ultimately turned into a less than happy story.

A Note on Board Duties

There is some value in creating a list of things you'd like each board officer to accomplish, although I wouldn't want to formally call it a "job description," particularly if your volunteers already have paying jobs. It's a good idea to create a document that designates board members duties and responsibilities, though. You'll want to vet them by matching their skills and expertise to the appropriate position. You can even add a "delivery date" if the board position requires that a specific task be completed within a given time frame (this could be particularly important in terms of website-related issues, for example). Be clear about expectations relating to attendance at meetings and tenure. Give prospective board members a hard copy of your bylaws to read before you formally ask them to join your board. After reviewing the bylaws, they may decide an officer position is not right for them but may be interested instead in taking on an understudy role to help out in a given capacity.

Job description or not, you will find that sometimes your officers just can't manage to get things done on time. In our organization, it's been my experience that the very few delays we've encountered are most often related to temporary familial challenges. I've found that by having an informal chat I can learn a little more about the issues that are delaying the work getting done, with the result that the work either gets re-prioritized or gets done by transferring the task to someone who can better fit it into his or her schedule.

I really rebel against the idea of asking your officers to sign contracts. "Managing by walking around" is an old concept here in Silicon Valley, and there's a reason it works. Your volunteer officers are involved because they want to be. It's fulfilling for them or they'd never be involved in the first place. I view contracts for volunteers as draconian measures that are endemic to a "top-down" rather than "flat" management style. The philosophy that works best for us lies in getting people to want to do something, rather than waving a contract in their faces and reminding them of an obligation that may no longer have meaning for them. Keep the lines of communication open, and you even can "walk around" by making telephone calls to your officers. Make sure your officers have fun and are doing something they enjoy, and continually emphasize how much they're contributing to the organization's mission.

In terms of raising money as it relates to your officers, I discuss the value of building a Keynote Program in the next chapter. You can bring all of your officers and many of your volunteers into the planning and implementation stages of such a program. And that creates funding. I believe it's important to have officers who believe in your mission and will do what needs to be done to make it succeed. Again, neither micromanaging nor dunning them for money individually has ever been preferred or required in our organization.

A number of books on the subject of nonprofits suggest multiday board retreats. But perhaps this is an expense you can do without. I advocate being in constant touch with your officers and having ad hoc meetings over a coffee or beer to discuss whatever can't be handled in a telephone conversation. A beer at Joe's is cheaper than a weekend at a resort. A counterargument is provided by Audrey Wong:

> I do think retreats (these can be as short as a half-a-day) are valuable. These are held separately from regular meetings or ad hoc gatherings. They are a way to get the whole board together for a time of communal reflection. How are we doing? Are we still on mission? Are we heading in the same direction? Are we heading in the right direction?[11]

If you elect to take Audrey's approach, I recommend you do it with an eye toward fiscal responsibility as well as consideration for your board members' time. Your donors may be more appreciative of the fact that your retreat was held at an affordable venue and kept to the objective at hand rather than at a high-end resort where your team engaged in pricey recreational activities.

Thanking Your Volunteers

I'm constantly thanking our volunteers for doing everything they do to keep our mission moving forward and enhancing our sustainability. There are lots of different ways for you to do the same. Once a year, we take our volunteer Board of Officers out to dinner, right after our board meeting. They can bring their spouses or partners, too. Occasionally I'll take volunteers to lunch to thank them and discuss their initiatives and ideas. Whatever means you use to thank someone, please do it in a way that will be appreciated. Not everyone likes balloons or award certificates, but some do. Everyone likes to eat, but not everyone eats the same thing (we have some vegetarians who are important volunteers). There are also important cultural aspects that I encourage you to consider. In many Asian cultures, for instance, being singled out for excellence in a public setting can be embarrassing, a philosophy that carries over to many (but not all) Asian-Americans as well.[12] My recommendation is to determine how people like to be thanked and take that into consideration, particularly if you're going public with it.

When Your Volunteers Leave

It's pretty common to have some degree of attrition when you're a volunteer operation. While your core volunteers and officers should be fairly stable in terms of their longevity with your organization, your younger volunteers will move on. On to college, paying jobs, moving out of state, or raising a family. Regardless of the reason, I'm always willing to write a recommendation, be a job reference, or do anything I can possibly do to help them move on to the next step in their lives. When yours leave, I encourage you to LinkIn to them, too, if you haven't already. You might be surprised at how giving them a great send-off will reward you in the future, by having them return to say hello occasionally, tell new acquaintances about how wonderful your organization was, or even get involved in a reunion a bunch of years later.

CHAPTER 7

Sponsorships: Building a Definitive, Self-Sustaining, Permanent and Exciting Keynote Program

A Keynote Program consists of an ongoing program or project that defines your mission and produces a kinetic action plan in which you, your officers, volunteers, and sponsors participate. It has to be self-sustaining or the eventuality of its permanence will be eroded. In the spirit of a nonprofit, you're engaging in an ongoing production that, in keeping with your mission, will be at the forefront of reaching your objectives. For many nonprofits, this program is the most significant resource of publicly generated revenue. The program must fund itself. It can take many forms. One local arts organization with which we're familiar is noted for its annual auction of artwork donated by local artists. A nearby neighborhood association hosts a one-day dog appreciation festival, rents out booths in a local park, and gets the lion's share of its yearly revenue that way. Your keynote program doesn't have to be a "walk-in" event either. It can occur on the Internet. And your Keynote Program can even *be* your nonprofit. The Cotati (California) Accordion Festival (www.cotatifest.com) occurs over an August weekend every summer, and here is its mission statement: "The Cotati Accordion Festival is a nonprofit organization, established in 1991, to promote the love of the accordion and to support local youth service organizations." Since its inception, it's given out more than $320,000 to local youth programs and schools. If the accordion can produce that amount of funding, think of what you can do with the ichigenkin!

You may not necessarily have a Keynote Program at the beginning, but you and your team should be thinking of one at the onset. It will not only give you focus but will also contribute to the success of your organization, both in making a contribution to your mission and for giving people a real reason to make a charitable contribution. I encourage you to strongly consider what individual donors will receive in return for their financial contributions. In my opinion, membership cards are virtually worthless, just more fodder for the trash can. But if you can give people something tangible, they'll contribute and tell their friends. In the examples I've given previously, donors get art, face time with other dog lovers, and an opportunity to be inundated with accordion bands.

In some cases, Keynote Programs will allow you to provide a tax deduction for your donors, others not. The IRS has rules about the fair-market value of what—if anything—a donor receives in return for a donation. In the accordion festival example, the donor gets a festival in return, the fair-market value of which is the price of the admission ticket. No tax write-off. On the other hand, if your Keynote Program involves a sponsorship in which nothing in terms of material goods accrue to the donor, you may be in a situation in which you can provide your donor with a tax deduction. As always, consult a tax professional or the IRS to determine where you stand.

Planning and Rapid-Prototyping Your Keynote Program

Although I believe in planning, I don't believe in ossification. You don't want to do so much planning that the inertia becomes unglued and the creators of the idea lose their initiative. Michael Patton, former Chairman of the American Evaluation Association, has an interesting quote in Steve Rothschild's book *The Non Nonprofit: For-Profit Thinking for Nonprofit Success*, in which he characterizes overplanning as a case of "Ready, aim, aim, aim, aim" when it really *should* be "Fire, learn, aim, fire, learn, aim."[1] I think Patton and Rothschild have a point. Your creative volunteers might mash up an idea for a keynote program and then blast it up on the website or Facebook to see what develops. In the software development world, this is known as *rapid prototyping,* generally a situation in which a user interface is cobbled together with some back-end stuff to link it to, then is released for internal review. It works, but not as well as it's going to work when it's fully done. It does, however, promote creativity, gives participants the satisfaction that the concept is doable, and is successful enough that such a process has resulted in numerous products that today are used by millions.

So here's a rapid-prototyping idea for you. Take three to five of your most creative volunteers and officers, and ask each to come up with an idea for a Keynote Program. You can set them up as a special Keynote Committee. As a prerequisite to being on the committee, I would recommend that you obtain agreement from them that they would all work on whichever Keynote Program that they collectively choose. The committee would then meet, listen to one another's ideas, then vote on them, each listing the best idea first, then ranking the order of next best, and so on. Each must vote for his or her idea as number one. The winning project could actually end up being the one that accrued the most number of votes as the second choice. The originator of the idea that is chosen gets to head the program as the Project Manager.

I'm an advocate of prototyping and launching a Keynote Program as soon as you get your notes on paper, your ideas discussed, and your challenges noted and solved. As a guerrilla nonprofit, you're expected to be aggressive, radical, and unconventional. Too many organizations take weeks to plan and implement, leaving the gung ho originators of the program frustrated. Particularly if you're a small nonprofit that runs solely on volunteers, you'll want your volunteers to know that their ideas for Keynote Programs can be transformed instantaneously into actions. For them, it's both rewarding and motivating to see things quickly move forward and gain momentum. Your Keynote Program won't be perfect as it leaves the starting gate. It will have bugs and glitches like all prototypes do. But because you and your team thought through potential problem areas, you'll fix them just as quickly as you launched the prototype, and every week the program will get a little more perfect.

As mentioned earlier, I'm a believer in the originator of the Keynote Program idea "owning" the project. In your initial discussions with the enthusiastic person who came up with the idea that was selected, ask him or her to describe the challenges of the program along with his or her solutions to those issues. Bring the Keynote Committee together again to brainstorm and think creatively to predict any other challenges that might occur.

Once the idea and Project Manager have been chosen, prototyping can begin, with a target date for a deliverable to the website, Facebook, or some other source available to the public. Your target date depends on your organization's facility with the public display technology. Putting something up on your website or other social media site shouldn't ideally take more than ten days from the committee's original meeting. That may seem aggressive, but as I mentioned in the "Building and Maintaining Your Website, E-mail, Social Media and Business-Networking Presence" and "Volunteers: Your Most Valuable Asset" chapters, you'll want to have volunteers conversant with building web pages and social media technologies.

Once it has presence on the website and social media, fully build out the remainder of the program. Ensure that there's a "call to action" element so visitors to your website or social media site know what they can do to donate or participate. And tell them what they get in return or what their contribution will provide. In the case of our Save A Film Keynote Program (discussed later), each sponsor got a DVD of the film he or she sponsored and was listed as the film's sponsor on the film's Internet Archive hosting page.

What donors receive doesn't necessarily have to accrue to them as a fixed asset, either. A very compelling Keynote Program was run by Interplast (now ReSurge International, www.resurge.org), an organization that performs reconstructive facial surgery for people in developing nations. Interplast advertised that for a fixed amount an individual in need of facial reconstruction would be selected in that donor's name and his or her donation would pay for the entire procedure. The one-on-one relationship, donor to recipient, was compelling: "Your donation pays for surgery that will change someone's life" is the tagline I remember.

Once your program is built out, officially launch it. After that, continually monitor it to gauge its success and tweak the program when necessary. Fine-tuning your Keynote Program is an iterative and ongoing process. Times and market realities change, and your program should adjust to them accordingly. Formally evaluate it every three months. Keep it if it works. If it's determined to be unsuccessful and not fixable, reengage the Keynote Committee and begin the process anew. But do remember that even a moderately successful program can be well worth keeping, even if it gets superseded by a new Keynote Program with bigger potential.

An Example of a Successful, Ongoing, Sustainable Keynote Program

Moving away from the purely theoretical, how does a nonprofit go about putting together a Keynote Program that's doable, successful, and sustainable? How will you identify problem areas early on and correct them before they delay or crash your project? How will you ensure that it aligns with your mission?

Our Keynote Program here at the AFA provides an example of how a typical nonprofit can grow a significant funding source from a relatively small initiative. As you read through the story, consider your own organization's potential or current Keynote Program and how you might be able to apply our experience to yours. The steps we took to develop a successful Keynote Program may be similar to the ones you'll take, in terms of how the program evolves and achieves success. You can do it, too, but you're encouraged not to wait as long as we did. Instead, if you don't yet have such a program, start thinking about it right away. Prototype it within ten days of deciding what it's going to do, whom it will serve, and how it will contribute to your mission. Once developed and activated, your Keynote Program should continue to pay for itself and provide additional needed funds as well. Do think "out of the box" and consider how other organizations and commercial entities might be able to partner with you. We did and got some fairly well-known commercial companies to cooperate with us and our sponsors.

We didn't exactly start with a bang. While maintaining focus on the elements of our mission statement, we didn't come up with a Keynote Program early on. We were doing public shows, the only program involving public interaction that we had. Most of our events attracted a maximum of twenty people. Many attendees would throw a small donation in a jar and got a show in return, so this didn't represent a tax deduction for them. Our mission was to prevent 16mm classroom films from destruction by saving them from landfills and showing them, thereby raising awareness as to the value of preserving them. But twenty isn't much of an audience. That would change in 2007 in a big way, with what became our Keynote Program. To get started, we had to take a serious look in the mirror.

Building a Keynote Program by Identifying and Fixing a Problem

We started with identifying a problem that needed to be fixed. For some time, people who visited our public film shows had been asking how they could view digitized versions of the films they saw. We liked that idea as well. This was problematic, though, as equipment to digitize films is expensive, the process of doing it can be labor-intensive, and none of our volunteers had digitization and uploading experience. In addition, we certainly didn't have the money to increase the server space and bandwidth on our website to host the films. There was also the issue of copyright clearance, somewhat less of a challenge because we were already in contact with many of the copyright holders. And overall, there was the funding problem. In a nutshell, here were our challenges:

1. No digitization equipment
2. No volunteers with digitization and uploading experience
3. Not enough storage space or bandwidth
4. Copyright clearance
5. No funding

Rick Prelinger, an eminent archivist, had advised us to consider uploading films to the Internet Archive (www.archive.org), an independent hosting site for films, among other things. That solved the storage and bandwidth issues. He recommended that we speak with Skip Elsheimer of AV Geeks (www.avgeeks.com), who had digitization equipment and was uploading some of the films in his own collection to the Internet Archive. Skip agreed to give us a significant discount as a nonprofit. That took care of the equipment and labor issues.

How Were We Going to Fund the Program and How Much Would We Charge?

We decided that we'd ask the people on our e-mail list to sponsor the digitization and uploading of films they liked. More than a thousand of such films had been programmed as part of our public shows, and film notes describing them were also available on our website. People could therefore sponsor a film they'd actually seen or choose one based on its description. Skip was going to charge us a fixed amount per foot of 16mm film he digitized, so for a ten-minute film, for example, we knew how much we'd pay him. Ten-minute films come in 400-foot cans, but not every 400-foot can holds films as long as ten minutes. They're often as short as four or five minutes. We didn't want to have to count the footage in each can of film and then have to calculate how much we'd charge for each film, which would have been extraordinarily labor-intensive. Instead, we came up with the idea that we'd just charge by can size. At $110 per 400-foot can, Skip would be paid and the film would be uploaded. If a film was fewer than 400 feet, we'd make a small profit to use for operating expenses, projector repair, and the usual other miscellaneous operating items. We set additional sponsorship levels for films in larger 800-foot and 1200-foot cans. This was an important consideration, as narrowing down the sponsor options to only four categories would make it easier for people to donate. We called our Keynote Program "Save A Film." Two days after we decided to launch the program, we prototyped two web pages that explained how it worked and how much it cost to sponsor a film (www.afana. org/saveafilm.htm).

So What Would the Sponsors Get?

One of the most rewarding aspects for the sponsors was that they'd get to see their sponsored films any time they wanted. They could tell their friends and even have a party in which everyone got to watch the film online. It would be up on the Internet and could be viewed anywhere, anytime, by anyone. Each donor would receive a DVD of his or her film, which had a material cost of $5. For a 400-foot film that they sponsored for $110, therefore, a sponsor would get a $105 tax deduction. We always make it a point to mail tax deduction confirmation letters to sponsors within a week of receiving their donations. These letters are mandatory for all donations exceeding $75 when donors receive goods or services in return (see the "Keeping the Government Happy" chapter). I add a small Post-it note to the donation letter, too, just to make it a little more personal.

Our Keynote Program became immediately successful. A good number of people who had attended our public shows began sponsoring the digitization and uploading of films. Filmmakers who wanted their films to be seen sponsored their own films (Academy Award nominee Carson Davidson guesses that more people have seen his films on our Internet Archive site than ever saw them in theaters). Families of filmmakers who had passed away sponsored their films as a memorial tribute to them. Subject matter that might be considered arcane, such as vintage foreign language instruction films made in the France of 1960, saw the light of day for the first time in decades.

We still had one problem, though. More than occasionally a copyright issue that prevented certain films from being uploaded. I bring this to your attention because there will be times that you'll encounter a challenge that initially may seem insurmountable from a legal perspective. With some creative thinking, though, you may be able to solve it and, in doing so, make your Keynote Program even stronger. Here's how we repositioned the problem, used a bit of creativity to solve it, and how the solution augmented and improved our program outcome.

Getting Corporate Entities to Buy into Our Keynote Program

Copyright ownership is always something to consider when making intellectual properties available for free public access and includes the broad areas of literature, music, and film. In our case, a classic example was the situation involving the exceptional academic classroom films made by Encyclopaedia Britannica, Inc. (EB). Our dilemma was that we wanted to digitize and upload many of them. They were most assuredly under copyright, and EB considered them valuable property. EB had made its last 16mm classroom film well before the end of the twentieth century, and while it still sold some of its films in video format, it hadn't converted very much of its massive catalogue to digital format. What film footage it had digitized was marketed through its business partner, Getty Images. We therefore approached EB with an idea. How about if we secured permission from EB to digitize and upload a finite number of selected films? We'd agree to send EB digital files of these films, which they could then repurpose into new DVDs to sell and also provide to Getty Images for footage rental. Our Keynote Program sponsorships would pay for all the digitization. We had a pretty good argument. If nobody ever saw the films, very few people would be aware of them, and if people weren't exposed to them, how would they ever use them or rent footage? As I explained to EB, our program was essentially a free marketing arm for them.

They agreed and we started small, with a few selected films. People started watching the EB films listed on our website as soon as the program was launched. Soon, documentary filmmakers and individuals representing commercial interests were making enquiries about licensing the films, which we forwarded to Getty Images. This gave both EB and Getty an opportunity to make a profit, and they joined us to describe the program at an Association of Moving Image Archivists conference, discussing how business and nonprofits could work together in a mutually beneficial relationship.

For all nonprofits, the takeaway here is to creatively consider how for-profit enterprises might be able to benefit in some material way by assisting you in accomplishing your organization's mission. If you decide to move in that direction, I strongly suggest "calling high" by calling into the executive level (e.g., President, CEO, or VP) of your target company, rather than starting with a lower-level individual. In many cases, you'll end up speaking with that executive's Executive Administrator and he or she will be able to get you to the most appropriate individual in the enterprise. Make sure you've already crafted your "here's what we can do for you" statement and can succinctly describe your mission statement. That's what we did.

Who Wins?

In a successful Keynote Program, everyone does. In the case of the Cotati Accordion Festival, schools do, the fans do, local people who sell food, drink, and materials do, and the musicians do. In our case at the AFA, filmmakers and families of filmmakers benefit and so do film companies and footage houses, individual sponsors, the public at large, and people and companies wanting to use and repurpose footage. We continually receive e-mails from teachers who are using this free content in their own underfunded classrooms as well.

Your Keynote Program brings you funding even when you can't get grants. It involves and energizes your public. It helps you to meet your mission's objectives. So go ahead and identify a problem associated with the goals of your nonprofit. Find a creative way to solve it, and develop an ongoing, self-funding keynote program that not only is fun and rewarding for your officers, volunteers, and public but also keeps you financially solvent on an ongoing basis.

Checklist

- Select volunteers and officers to be on the Keynote Committee, who agree to build a rapid prototype of their winning Keynote Program idea.
- The committee meet and choose the idea.
- Prototype it on the website and/or social media within ten days.
- Fully build out the remainder of the program. Ensure that there's a "call to action" element so visitors to your website or social media site know what they can do to donate or participate. And tell them what they get in return or what their contribution will provide.
- Continually monitor its success and tweak the program when necessary.
- Evaluate it every three months. Keep it if it works. If it's determined to be unsuccessful and not fixable, reengage the Keynote Committee and begin the process anew.
- Encourage everyone in your organization to keep coming up

with new Keynote Program ideas. Don't think that you have to run everything through the committee, either. If the idea is vetted and doable, why not just let the originator prototype it and run with it?

CHAPTER 8

Events, Benefits, Conferences and Nontraditional Ways to Pay a Few Bills

Public exposure through face-to-face interaction is a key to publicizing your mission and educating the public, acquiring donations, and developing e-mail and (if you choose to go that route) postal mailing lists. Events include those you host yourself as well as others in which you participate. Events can be one-off or ongoing. Your alliances, volunteers, and sponsors can host benefits for you as well, and you'll want to be aware of organizations and interest groups that hold conferences and seminars that are particular to your field of interest. Conferences and seminars are wonderful places to stage events that can elevate the public profile of your organization.

Since your nonprofit may not attract funding organizations that see your value, you may very well want to seek some source of funding that will at least pay for daily office consumables like paper clips, laser printer toner, and postage. Think creatively. Events and benefits can be great fun for your volunteers, hosts, and attendees. They can be important in your overall funding scheme, but they can lose a lot of money, too, if you go overboard in laying out too much money up front. Here are some aspects you'll want to consider as you think through the possibilities.

Try to Avoid Paying Rent for an Event Venue

In staging events and benefits, there are a few things we learned along the way that helped us to accrue as much funding as possible from them while keeping expenses low. The first one was, whenever possible, to avoid paying rent for facilities. A good nontraditional way to do this is to hold your event or benefit in a bar or restaurant, and ensure that the owners of your hosting venue make some money when you do. If they make money, you'll be welcomed back to hold another event. At the AFA, our initial public events were film shows. We approached the Agenda Lounge, a local bar and restaurant that had an underground speakeasy with tables and chairs and a bar but typically didn't open downstairs for patrons until 11:00 p.m. We suggested running a film program from 7:00 to 10:00 p.m. and instead of having the Agenda pay a bar employee to run the speakeasy bar, we'd instead ask our attendees to buy their drinks upstairs and bring them down to the speakeasy themselves. Our visitors could also arrive early at 6:00 p.m. and buy dinner, too. Because it involved no expense and provided profit deriving from a space that was not generating revenue, the Agenda management enthusiastically let us have the space. Since our shows were free of charge, we just passed the hat for donations and people could give whatever they liked. We did more than 400 shows there. The bar and restaurant made a lot of money from our patrons, and since they didn't need to hire additional personnel, it was pure profit for them. We did well on donations, so it was a win-win. The venue cost us nothing.

We've always resisted getting involved in situations where there was the possibility of financial risk, and usually that begins with a rental fee that may not be equaled or exceeded if you don't reach a certain dollar amount in donations. In your situation, I'd encourage you to look around in your community for a venue that is already open, has tables and chairs, but isn't using its space as profitably as it could be. If you're staging regular events, you might find it easier to convince your venue to give you space rent-free by staging it on a non-weekend night, when it could use some extra business. In addition to our main venue, we staged shows at several other restaurants and art galleries. The way we approached the management of these venues was similar each time: "You get the bar and food revenue and we'll ask for donations." The organization donating the space can also do it as an "in-kind" donation, in which they valuate you rental at their usual rate, donate the space to you, and you provide them with a donation letter that they can use as a potential tax write-off, indicating date, time, place, hours, and financial value.

In addition to bars and restaurants, we presented our public domain films in special shows at several theatres as well. In these cases, they paid us a fixed fee and collected admission by ticket. Again, everyone won.

Making Lemonade Out of a Lemon:
Losing Your Free Space and
Landing on Your Feet

As will be addressed in the next chapter, "Working the Big Room: Building Alliances and Affiliates," it's important to establish communication with organizations and businesses with whom you can create mutually beneficial relationships. Because you never know when you might lose your free rental space. And if you do lose the space, make sure you do everything possible to maintain a good relationship with that organization. If you walk away without burning bridges, you just might be invited back. Even if you're not, you'll enhance your reputation as a class organization, which may very well encourage others to want to work with you.

We had just such a situation and here's how we dealt with it. The owner of the Agenda Lounge (see previous section) had graciously agreed to give us his underground cellar space on Thursday nights for our free film shows. We turned it into a real speakeasy, where people could smoke, drink, and watch films. Part of the agreement, as I said, was that our visitors would buy dinners and drinks from the Agenda, carry them downstairs, and enjoy the films. One night, a problem occurred that brought everything to a halt. One of our crazy attendees (we had several) brought in his own dinner from a nearby fast-food restaurant. The Agenda owner asked him not to do that and suggested he leave until he'd finished his fast-food meal outside. The attendee in question further exacerbated the situation by getting involved in a heated argument with the owner. The next day, the owner asked to meet me, and the end result was that we were asked to leave. The approach I took was to thank him for being a patron of the arts and hosting us for as long as he did. The space he'd provided us was invaluable to the success of our shows, and I really was grateful. We shook hands, and I began looking for another venue. Later, I was to find that he was surprised that my response to the whole thing was to thank him. He wasn't used to being thanked. It wasn't difficult, because he had been a patron and we understood his position. We had a diverse audience and the behavior of some of our audience members could be, at times, unpredictable. If you're open to involving the public at large in your events, you'll encounter occasional problems such as this as well.

We immediately found another venue and we made the same agreement. The restaurant/bar got all the food and drink proceeds. It wasn't, however, as fun and offbeat as the Agenda space. A year later, though, the Agenda owner called me out of the blue. He wanted us back. It was perfect timing, as the manager at our newer venue had wanted to fill our space with a new venture. So we thanked him enthusiastically, moved back to the Agenda, and stayed there for several more years until we stopped doing public shows.

This story underscores two important concepts that you'll want to keep in mind. First, if your nonprofit deals with the public, you'll run into folks that love you but will cause problems for you in your dealings with others. You'll want to think ahead and know how you'll react when such a situation occurs. Second, strive to maintain great relationships within your business and nonprofit community and thank everyone all the time, even when the relationship runs into rocky shoals. If you've got a reputation of being easy to work with, people will want to work with you.

Events: Be Innovative and Create a Buzz

Use your team's creativity in coming up with the theme for an event and you can come up with some crazy ideas that will create press publicity and bring people in the door. Don't be afraid to poke fun at yourself, either. A few years ago, the nonprofit San Jose Art League staged such an event that also served as a benefit. For years, local artists had been donating their paintings to the Art League, and these eventually filled up the entire basement, creating a storage problem. Lots of this work was marginal and some of the artwork was, everyone agreed, just plain horrible (the artists had received tax breaks for donating their work). But, of course, art is in the eye of the beholder. So the Art League staged a "San Jose Art: The Best and the Worst" show. They told the press that they'd show some of their finest pieces as well as horrific examples of terrible art and got publicity from the local newspapers. As it turned out, everybody wanted to see the bad art. Jack Nyblom, the owner of a well-known local film theater, provided a quote that was used on the flyer: "I don't want to make enemies, but this is something you'd see on a greeting card ... moves me to semi-nausea." It was juxtaposed with another tongue-in-cheek quote from Joel Tansey, noted scholar and son of the well-regarded art historian Richard Tansey: "This is the greatest art this country has seen since the Armory Show of 1931." Everything in the show could be purchased, for prices ranging from $5 to $50 (this memorable event was staged in 1986). Concerned and occasionally angry artists telephoned the Art League when they initially heard about the show, asking if their donated works were listed among the "best" or "worst." The Art League was cagey enough to respond by telling them they'd have to come to the show to see for themselves. But it was smart. It displayed everything, categorized nothing into "best" and "worst" labels, and let the visitors decide for themselves. Most of the art was sold, the event represented a significant financial success, and valuable storage space was regained. As a result of the press interest, loads of new people found out about the Art League, bought artwork, joined the e-mail list, and became members. And people were talking about how much fun they'd had for months to come.

Your organization's take-away from the Art League experience is that one person's junk is another's gold and you might be able to take material you have lying around, get a little creative, and use it for an event that can generate publicity and funding. Here's yet another approach.

If you're an organization with a membership, you can stage fundraising events that include only your members, too. Monterey (CA) Peninsula College Printmakers is an organization that provides facilities for local artists to make prints. Occasionally, they'll have a members-only fund-raiser in which each member pays $10 and donates one print. All prints are displayed with an identification number. A hat is passed, and one person picks a number. He or she then is the owner of the corresponding print. The person whose print has been chosen is allowed to pick from the hat next, and so on. The event only takes one hour, and $300 to $400 is raised each time it is staged, derived from the $10 entry fee.

Staging Benefits

One of the most compelling reasons for you to stage ongoing events is that your attendees may very well offer to hold benefits for you. We have developed close relationships with many of our event attendees, several of whom then became our most valuable volunteers. Several others offered to host benefits for us in their homes. This was a wonderful perk, as not only did we raise a good amount of funding, but we also were able to host a great film show in the backyard of a beautiful home. We advertised the benefit through our e-mail list, asking for a suggested donation along with an RSVP so we could determine how many people would attend. We bought red and white wine, beer, soda pop, and water and, again, asked for a suggested donation for drinks. Our hosts rented some inexpensive plastic chairs.

The best benefits I've attended include those hosted by Rick Holden and Sandy Moll, two local arts benefactors. They've opened their home to benefits for numerous nonprofits and part of the reason for their success is that these benefits are fun and they're affordable for just about everybody. Rick notes some key elements of making a benefit work well:

> We have an exotic backyard space, so people always like to come and enjoy it. We make sure we have a few different kinds of beer and two varieties each of red and white wine. The wine is good, but not expensive, and we rarely pay more than $15 a bottle. The organization for whom we're holding the benefit or event always has a speaker, and our oratory rule is to make it short, usually no more than fifteen minutes, just so he or she can say, "Here's why we're here," and, "Here's what you can do to

help." People are here for fun, not to listen to long speeches. Another rule is that people coming to our events and benefits don't have to buy anything or make an auction bid. We tell them up front how much of a donation is requested. That way, people don't feel they're being strong-armed, and it's simple and fun, for us, the donors, and the organization.[1]

Sandy adds:

I would also add that it is nice to do a donor recognition event in a home or garden that people are interested in seeing. Much nicer than a hotel room and makes for a greater draw. At these events, the talk is all about the "thank you" and then either Rick or I talk about why we support the organization and/or the Executive Director talks about how the donors' support has helped the organization and/or what the upcoming initiatives are that need continued or new support—still keeping all this to 15 minutes max. There is no "ask" per se, but there may be return envelopes and information available as people leave.

When these are held in our garden, the organization provides all the food and beverages usually, but not always. Sometimes we will underwrite it. In any case, we always use local caterers who will give us a "deal" because they are supportive of the community and/or us. And, as Rick said, the beverages are good but not expensive. We have wine glasses for up to 60 people which we have purchased at Cost Plus World Market at very reasonable prices. Then we try to keep the use of plates to a minimum and have nice paper napkins. Sometimes we rent plates and utensils, but not often.[2]

Here in California, nonprofits can usually host outdoor events all year around. But if your climate doesn't allow for that, consider building a fun and informative video or slide show presentation, musical performance, or lecture and ask your volunteers or those on your e-mail list if they'd enjoy hosting an event in their homes on a winter evening. In our experience, many of our wealthier contacts with large homes love to sponsor occasional events, particularly at the time of year, typically after Labor Day and before Memorial Day, when a benefit event held in their homes is a welcome diversion during the cooler months.

Announcing Your Event or Benefit

Essentials in terms of announcing your event include Evites, e-mail, your website, news and broadcast media public service announcements (PSAs), and social media. These days, Evite (www.evite.com) has made event announcements and RSVPs a snap. This free web application is easy to use and your invitees get to make comments, too, which adds a social media element that provides a nice dimension. You'll also want to make announcements to your e-mail list. But use caution here in terms of how often you contact those on your list. People don't need or want more than one Evite or e-mail event announcement per event per week. So if you've loaded your e-mail list into your Evite list, ensure that you make it no more than once per week. A couple of friends of mine host an enormous yearly art party every year that benefits our art community. But when their Evites went out twice per week, they got plenty of complaints. People felt overwhelmed and aggravated.

Add your event announcement to the home page of your website, and include an RSVP link in the announcement for responses. And ensure that you create press releases and send them to your local radio, television, and newspaper outlets as PSAs. Don't forget local community and college radio stations, either, as some of your most significant donors may make it a habit of listening to commercial-free radio.

Finally, you will want to include an event announcement on your Facebook, LinkedIn, and any other social media pages. If you don't have these, visit the "Volunteers: Your Most Valuable Asset" chapter and identify a volunteer who embraces social media and is enthusiastic about creating and maintaining a page for your organization.

A Note About Advertising

I learned the hard way about advertising as it relates to small enterprises. Some time back, I co-owned a retail establishment that was sustaining itself nicely. One day, a radio adman suggested that we do a radio campaign. We spent some money, got a few new customers as a result of it, but couldn't justify the cost of the campaign. The return on investment (ROI) just wasn't there. Our ad exec suggested we try rewording and reworking, so we did. Same results. So he suggested we rework and test the campaign again. We said no. If we followed his advice, we'd probably still be testing and spending. And that is the nature of the advertising business: if it doesn't work, just spend more money. Today, with your website, social media, e-mail, PSAs, and all the other publicity options open to you, there are plenty of things your nonprofit can do to generate interest without the money sink of ongoing advertising campaigns.

Conferences

I encourage you to become a member of an organization that encompasses your nonprofit's area of expertise and attend its yearly conference. The first year, you'll be busy meeting new people and chatting up your organization. Meet as many officers of the hosting organization as you can, and start thinking about what you could present at next year's conference that would add to the general knowledge of the people attending. You may very well come up with a great idea for your own potential presentation during your first day or so at the conference, so float it by everyone you can to judge how others relate to it as a presentation topic. Make it your objective at your first conference to collect as many business cards as you can (be sure to write notes on the reverse) and come away with a topic that you'll suggest presenting next year.

As soon as the conference is over, start making notes on your proposed conference topic right away, before you forget anything. In some cases, you'll need to have other experts on your panel, so contact them and come up with a plan. In several months, you'll be able to submit a conference proposal, and you'll already have the topic and co-presenters selected. This is precisely what we did when we attended our first Association of Moving Image Archivists (AMIA) conference. Since our first conference, we've made a number of subsequent presentations and have also shown several of the films in our collection on the Archival Screening Night, a highlight of each year's conference.

Our relationship with AMIA has resulted in elevating the perception of our small archive to others in the archival community. Its members have connected us to a number of film libraries that were being deaccessioned, several of which were donated to us, thus improving the depth and scope of our collection. AMIA members have also become important colleagues to us, as we swap information, ask and answer questions, and cooperate throughout the year.

Determining which organization's conference is best for you can be a critical element in terms of elevating your presence and importance within your nonprofit's area of expertise. Do a web search on your organization's area of expertise or focus audience and you may find several. As a nonprofit with an eye to sustainability, you may choose to avoid the more expensive ones. Price does not always equate to the quality of the conference in terms of your objectives. You can save money in other ways, too. Many conferences are held in upscale hotels, but that doesn't mean you have to stay there. Often, the money you save by staying in less expensive lodging will pay for your conference fees, transportation costs, and food.

Here's a short checklist of ideas you want to strongly consider, in terms of events, benefits, and conferences.

Checklist

- Host a series of ongoing events at rent-free venues.
- Convene a benefit at the home of a sponsor or volunteer.
- Attend a conference specific to your area of expertise.
- Craft a proposal and submit it so that you can make a presentation at the following year's conference.

CHAPTER 9

Working the Big Room: Building Alliances and Affiliates

So you're a tiny nonprofit in a small town, hundreds of miles away from the largest city. Few people know about you, although you have your website up. How are you going to get some "juice" to elevate the importance of your work? "Work the Big Room" by establishing relationships with organizations that have people like you in them and who care about similar things. For your Rafflesia flower, you've got local, state, national, and international horticultural organizations. Your ichigenkin nonprofit can hook into string music societies and ethnomusicology organizations. Your glass telephone pole insulator organization can begin communicating with mass communication historical museums and technology-based historical societies. Don't forget ethnicities, either. Rafflesia may very well interest Malaysian and Indonesian interest groups, and ichigenkin will have value for Japanese and Nisei organizations.

You "work the room" by contacting folks at these organizations. Send them to your website, point them to your writings and white papers, join their organizations, and attend their conferences. This is an essential way of broadcasting your mission and expertise among people who will value it. Sometimes a potential affiliate or alliance partner will have a program that helps you to achieve one or more of the objectives listed in your mission statement, and often that organization will find you through another affiliate partner or your website. Establishing a network of affiliates and alliances can do wonders for making your nonprofit successful.

9. *Working the Big Room*

Here at the AFA, among a number of organizations with whom we interact, there are two in particular that we consider to be major alliances. Let me tell you about them, with the idea that you might consider replicating, specific to your own area of interest, what we did.

Our Relationship with AMIA

An organization that resonated with me initially was the Association of Moving Image Archivists (AMIA). Its membership consists of media archives and archivists from around the world, and as I mentioned earlier, they have a yearly conference in the United States. I read about them online, liked what I saw, bought myself a lifetime membership, then started planning for my first AMIA conference. Beforehand, I made sure our website was as spiffy and informative as I could make it. I printed a bunch of business cards with our sexy new logo. And a big part of the job, I realized, was repositioning myself, as the director, from being a "collector" to an "archivist." I've got a decent educational background, but my degrees aren't in media studies or film history. Many AMIA members are scholars in noted educational institutions, and it was important to promote the work we were doing as a resource for educational professionals and media historians. As ours was a newer and therefore largely unknown organization, gaining credibility with others in the field was critical.

When I attended the AMIA conference, I shook hands and gave out business cards to everyone I met. Everyone. No one knew who were at the beginning of the conference, but hundreds did afterward. We were dealing with what was then an arcane corner of film history that had been untouched by most scholars: 16mm classroom films made on Science and Humanities subjects. So I had to quickly explain both the importance of these films as well as the critical element of ensuring that they weren't thrown into landfills. As I had anticipated, many people I talked to equated educational films with school bus safety and hygiene. I also wanted to elevate this perspective by repositioning how people thought about these films. This is what you'll have to do to change the perception of the Rafflesia as just a "stinky flower," the ichigenkin as an instrument with limited harmonic range, or telephone pole insulators as mere pieces of glass that are best melted down and repurposed as glass bottles.

Our Relationship with History San José

Our nonprofit started getting inundated with film donations after we attended our first AMIA conference. If you "work the room" with alliances as I suggested, you may be very well faced with how you're going to handle donations of materials, from books to films to periodicals to other ephemera. And you're going to have to catalogue it, store it, maybe photograph it, too. Right after we began our process to be a nonprofit, we ran into David Crosson, who was at that time the CEO of History San José (HSJ), our local history museum (www.historysan jose.org). He was thrilled with our concept and offered us fifty feet of linear storage space at HSJ's collection center. Our agreement was that we'd provide films from our collection to support HSJ's exhibitions in return for the space. It costs money for films to be digitized, but we soon found sponsors willing to help with that (see the "Sponsorships: Building a Definitive, Self-Sustaining, Permanent and Exciting Keynote Program" chapter). Alida Bray, who succeeded Dave as CEO, is just as enthusiastic about the partnership, and Collections Manager Ken Middlebrook and Jim Reed, Curator of Archives and Library, provide constant support and continual ideas on how our films can support HSJ's mission as well. Whenever they mount an exhibition, they ask us to supply films that can run in the exhibition space on a continual basis, and most of the time we can help. Yet another organization, the California Pioneers of Santa Clara County (www.californiapioneers.com), cooperates with us by digitizing select films free of charge, in conjunction with HSJ. The end result is that HSJ and the Pioneers get digitized copies of some our films for public exhibitions and documentation purposes. And we have archival space that is essentially a trade-out, in return for in-kind media services. So think big, think out of the box, and you can obtain important exhibition or archival space from local public entities and nonprofits at no cost to you in return for assisting them in meeting their objectives.

I encourage you to put some effort into lending your assistance and cooperation to organizations and companies that support your mission and telling them about the important work you're doing. The Library of Congress (LOC) and the Academy of Motion Picture Arts and Sciences Film Archive are just two of these with whom we here at the AFA have collaborated, in terms of assistance in adding films to their own collections or in film preservation efforts. If your nonprofit needs to ask for occasional favors, donations, space, or people, a worthy amount of prestige can be gained from a little name-dropping, too, so consider spreading your contact net far and wide. Don't settle for e-mail introductions all the time, either. Call them and establish a personal relationship and invite them to connect to you on LinkedIn. As you build your alliance and affiliate network, you'll find that mentioning the names of them will ease your path forging a relationship with others.

Working with For-Profit Corporate and Public Affiliates

As I mentioned in the "Sponsorships: Building a Definitive, Self-Sustaining, Permanent and Exciting Keynote Program" chapter, we've developed a reputation of helping others to be successful, either in achieving their missions becoming more financially profitable. Even when we accrue no profit ourselves. Most people who create nonprofits are doing it to make the world a better place. And when we can help companies become more profitable by helping us in our mission, we'll do that, too. I've already mentioned our working relationship with Encyclopaedia Britannica and Getty Images. But they're not the only ones. We also have similar relationships with companies such as Scholastic and Pyramid Media. The key to making these relationships successful is understanding how your organization can be of assistance to them and, during your discussions, focusing on their perspective, not yours. Corporations and institutions are often inundated with nonprofits asking for things. By offering something of value instead, you'll position your organization as being different from many of the other nonprofits that approach them for assistance. And when you offer something, you'll often be regarded as a potentially valuable partner, rather than an organization just looking for a handout.

CHAPTER 10

Publicity and Publishing: Getting Others to Know About Your Work

As a sustainable nonprofit, you don't have to pay for publicity. Publicity can be derived in a number of effective ways, but publishing, in one form or another, can play a significant role in getting the word out about your organization. Three of my favorite ways to get publicity are to get interviewed on the radio, on television, and in the newspapers. And speaking publicly about your work in clubs and societies has value, too. If you don't think you're a public speaker, you can change that. Enroll in your local Toastmasters group (www.toastmasters.org) and you'll be a better speaker in a very short amount of time. The skills you pick up there will last a lifetime. You can also identify a volunteer or officer who loves to speak in public and you can work together to find venues.

Clubs and Societies

You will have local clubs and societies that just love having speakers come in for a lunch presentation. So think of musical societies for the ichigenkin, technology societies for glass insulators, and botanical and garden groups for Rafflesia. Do think big. We have a fairly well-known film festival here called Cinequest. I made contact with them, and one year they asked me to be a judge. The next year they invited me to bring in Richard Leacock, a noted documentarian whose work we'd ourselves shown. Those two appearances got us loads of free publicity.

Radio and Television

As a small nonprofit, ensure that every small local radio and television station and newspaper knows about you. You might think it's hard to get on the radio. It isn't. Most commercial radio stations have a public affairs person who loves to fill up airtime with interesting material. The Federal Communications Commission mandates that radio stations do some form of public affairs broadcasting to keep their license in order. Particularly if you have an offbeat story that makes "good radio," the public affairs people will listen to you. Describe to them what makes your organization unique and why it might interest their listeners. Pay special attention to radio stations that you listen to yourself. And whatever you do, don't forget about college and non-commercial radio stations. Doing an interview on a college station may result in your getting great volunteers as well. When we started doing our public film shows, we started with only one volunteer. Robert Emmett was a host for an outstanding public affairs show on KFJC, a local community radio station. I called him and he gave us an interview. That resulted in quite a few new people attending our shows. Robert himself became a volunteer for us almost immediately as our PR Officer and gave us an interview on his program at least once a year. We've appeared on a number of other radio stations as well. Radio stations love us in particular because we're enthusiastic, different, and fun and that makes good radio.

You should consider community television outlets as well. Just make a call. Jan Wahl, a well-known film reviewer on KCBS Radio, invited us to appear on her community television show. Again, think what makes for great television. It most often includes visuals, so tell your prospective host about how you'll show off your one-string zither from Japan, your outstandingly beautiful glass insulators, or how you'd like them to come down and shoot footage of the beautiful exotic flower that others dread, but you love.

Don't worry about prime time for either radio or television, and realize that you're probably going to get aired on Sunday morning or late at night. It doesn't matter, as loads of people are watching and listening, even then.

The Press

You'll have a great story to tell, but your major daily might not be interested. Call them anyway. The *San Jose Mercury News*, our big daily, never gave us an interview, but they did publish our weekly film listings, and the art columnist gave us publicity every time we staged an event or benefit. You may have local weekly alternative newspapers, and in my experience they're the best for giving you great publicity. They're fighting for readers against the big guys and love material that the dailies won't cover. Richard Von Busack, the film critic for the weekly San Jose *Metro*, wrote about us constantly, and we even got a cover story once. The alternative press has an alternative audience, and they appreciate hearing about unusual, out-of-the-box events and programs.

Your World of Publishing

I'm a real believer in publishing material germane to the topic of your nonprofit's mission. It creates a publicity buzz, which will go a long way to driving interest in sponsorships for your Keynote Programs and acquiring other donations. You already know enough about your subject matter to have decided to build a nonprofit around it, so you must at least publish to your website and create a newsletter. You can also write white papers and journal articles, but there's nothing like a book to display your expertise and publicize your organization. I encourage you to "think big" on this topic. So you're not a writer? Then make it a priority to acquire an officer or volunteer who loves to write and who is willing to take responsibility for writing your periodical newsletter. Here are some publishing ideas, beginning with the simplest.

Write an Ongoing Newsletter

Your newsletter is a periodically written house organ that keeps your subscribers up to date on your news and events. Although you may want to go through the expense of printing it and sending it by mail, so many people have e-mail these days that I'd recommend sending it that way to keep expenses at a minimum. Another great advantage of e-mail newsletters is that readers can click on links embedded in your e-mail, particularly advantageous when you make a brief request for donations (see the "Building and Maintaining Your Website, E-mail, Social Media and Business-Networking Presence" chapter for easy instructions on creating a "Donation" button).

How often should your newsletter appear? At least as often as you have events (we published ours weekly to announce our shows), but once a month at least. Ensure that you contact your local media outlets and secure their e-mail addresses. Here are some important guidelines to consider as you write your e-mail newsletter:

E-MAIL BEST PRACTICES

1. Poor spelling and grammar can reflect unfavorably on the professionalism of your organization. Use your spell-checker and proofread at least twice. Spell-checkers are not always completely reliable, so ask another person to read it as well.

2. Many people today are reading e-mail on smartphones and other PDAs (personal digital assistants). Use 10-point Arial print, therefore, and avoid the use of graphics.

3. In the subject line, leave a short, compelling, interest-getting message. Be brief.

4. Brevity is appreciated by people that receive many e-mails per day. Ideally, your newsletter, therefore, should consist of no more than one page.

5. Try to include no more than two links to web pages. Too many links can be confusing.

6. Mention an activity that will represent a call to action. This could be an event or an invitation to join in on your keynote sponsorship program. Free stuff can be compelling. If you have a "giveaway" (ours are free films they can see on the web), mention it early.

7. Make templates out of commonly sent e-mails so you won't have to continually reinvent the wheel. A good idea is to use the previous e-mail newsletter as a template, then edit it with your new information. And be sure to change the date to reflect the current calendar.

8. "Soft-pedal" your donation requests. If you consistently use newsletters as nothing more than requests for money, people will con-

sider your newsletters to be spam and won't read them anymore. Always lead your newsletter with informatively interesting, newsworthy content. I'd place the donation request as the last item in your newsletter.

9. Be courteous. Make it easy for people to unsubscribe by providing that option at the bottom of your e-mail newsletter.

Publish to Your Website

In addition to your own white papers, you can publish material from other authors on your website once you receive permission from them. In our own case at the AFA, we started finding interviews with filmmakers that hadn't seen public view in years and put them up on our website. Some of them, like notable filmmaker Richard Leacock's interview with silent screen star Louise Brooks, were outrageous and sexy (www.afana.org/leacockessays.htm#AConversationwithLouise Brooks). Ricky was enthusiastic about having it appear on our website, too, and gave us lots of additional material. Eventually, he used our website as a template to build his own and linked back to us, which gave us additional publicity and visitors. You might be surprised at how many will want to contribute to your website. Marsha Gordon teaches a film history class for graduate students at North Carolina State University and asked us to recommend some filmmakers for her students to interview. When the interviews were finished, we published them all on our website.

Publish a White Paper or Journal Article

A white paper is an authoritative topic-specific document that assists people in understanding a problem or issue. If you have your data at hand, you might be able to easily write it in a day or two. It might be a treatise on how to tune (and keep in tune) an ichigenkin or how to grow and maintain Rafflesia or be specific to historical manufacturers of glass insulators. Just like a book, you can quote from others, citing references while stating your own opinions. You may even have a collection of past material you've written, including articles of yours that were published in newspapers, magazines, and newsletters, some of which might possibly be crafted into white papers themselves. You can publish white papers directly to your website, and eventually they might even form the core of your book.

Are there any academic or trade journals specific to your area of expertise? I'd strongly advise you to consider contributing to them. The first paper I ever got published was through *The Moving Image*, the journal of the Association of Moving Image Archivists. One advantage of publishing through the journal was that I got a terrific editor, Christopher Horak, who made cogent suggestions that improved the article tremendously. I retained copyright and was later able to use the article, in edited format, in my first book.

Write a Book

You can either write it yourself or stage a collaborative effort with other experts, some of whom may be your officers or volunteers. Books today don't even have to have a formal publisher, as you can self-publish through print-on-demand (POD) companies or develop an eBook. Unless you're a stone-cold academic, I wouldn't encourage you to write in a scholarly style, but instead write as you speak, telling lots of stories and anecdotes to emphasize your points (I once told a publisher that you'd never see the word "hegemony" in any of my books—oops, I just used it!). Write what you yourself would like to read and in a manner that resonates with you.

If you elect to opt for a formal publishing house, find one that publishes material similar to yours and in writing styles compatible with the way you write. My first book was a history of academic classroom film, and I wrote it for archivists like me who were trying to figure out more about the people and companies that made these films. It got turned down by a number of university presses, most of whom wanted a chronological narrative in a more scholarly format. Fair enough, but I don't write like that, and I don't particularly want to read material like that, either. Eventually, I found a small but well-regarded publisher (McFarland) that had published a lot of books on film subjects and pop culture. I wrote up a proposal and they took my manuscript.

Getting a book published will assist greatly in publicizing your organization and may give you additional "juice" with volunteers, affiliates, organizations, and funders as well. If the idea of writing a book seems daunting, start writing a bit at a time. Whenever you get an idea, type it up, store it in a "book" file in your computer, and you're on your way. What have you written before? Back before our nonprofit days I wrote film notes for hundreds of shows we did, and later I mined that material pretty heavily for my book. I'd already done the work, written it up, and lots of it was sitting there on the website but not collected and collated yet into a format that made sense for a formal book. It took some reworking, but much of that material did get used.

Can't find a publisher? Today, that's not a huge problem. You can self-publish via a print-on-demand platforms such as those offered by Blurb (www.blurb.com), CreateSpace (www.createspace.com), and Lulu (www.lulu.com), where you don't even have to carry inventory and instead can print according to your need and then sell your books on a website such as Amazon. The end result can look surprisingly good. The fees for these services, though, can mount up, especially in the book design phase. For that reason, I recommend that you spend some time identifying and contacting formal book publishers first. A good way to narrow the list is to visit both new and used bookstores, go to the stacks corresponding to your area of expertise, and write down the names of publishing houses that produce books similar to the one you'll write.

Print-on-demand companies and customer service is variable, so if you go that route some due diligence is required. Here are two radically different experiences, one troublesome, the other terrific.

On the one hand, Jan Everote utilized the services of one such company to publish a print-on-demand book of her father's film industry memoirs[1]:

> Having completed the lengthy process of self-publishing between August 2012 and July 2013, I cannot honestly recommend ... [this company] unless one has endless patience and can operate without any real assistance. Since I had no publishing experience, we purchased the highest level publishing package in order to have the best quality paper, cover, print and the most customer service. Judging by our experience, I shudder to think how the lower level service clients must have been treated.
>
> Their stated 6 month time frame turned into almost 1 year ... by no fault of ours. We had great difficulty communicating with our lead person, and she ultimately quit when we were almost finished with the book.

10. Publicity and Publishing

It was obvious that she was totally overworked and she admitted that many others in her position had quit, increasing her work load. Edits were difficult as they kept dropping the changes I had made, saved and returned to them. Timing was a joke as the standard e-mail line was we'll get back to you in 3–5 business days and it would end up being 3 weeks. Pictures were submitted in the early stage as requested and then never seen again, even in the galley print. This, even though I kept asking to review them and the captions, and questioning how we could go to galley print without the photos. In fact, they had lost them, so we had to resend them. Captions were dropped and everything that went back to them took forever, no matter how minor.

The best work was done initially when the editorial recommendation was to move from present tense to past tense. They made those changes and they were well done. Beyond that, grammatical cleanup was useful, but tempered by the fact that the edits we saved turned up wrong again when the manuscript was returned for the next step. I should also mention they assume that you understand everything about the edit boxes as no instruction was ever given, nor was there on any other aspect of the process. On a final note, the paperbacks had a better quality paper, and the picture resolution was far superior to the hard cover books we received. When queried on this, their response was "nothing we can do, that is the way it is." Enough said.[2]

On the other hand, novelist Raymond F. Cavanagh[3] had an outstanding publishing experience with CreateSpace after a less-than-successful effort with his first choice:

As a first time novelist, I had a desire to submit my work through traditional methods, either directly to a publisher or through a literary agent. I had been warned that it was extremely difficult for a first time writer to achieve success in that manner, but felt I had a chance. I sent out query letter after query letter and accumulated rejections by the dozen. I decided to look into the process and publish on my own. Having worked in the technology industry for over 30 years, I felt that it would be fairly easy to use the online tools, publish the book and become an instant success. Boy was I wrong!

My first order of business was to identify which web site to use to self-publish. I did the usual web searches and found that opinions varied widely on what was the best tool, ease of use, and support in both front end (creative) and back end (marketing). I had been told of a web site that was one of the early entries in the field of self-publishing, and decided to sign up and try it.

First, let me point out that virtually all of the sites I visited were trying to sell me something. But I was stubborn. I wanted to do it all myself and not have to pay anyone. Consider that I went into this venture not intending to publish at all, but after ongoing encouragement from my first readers, decided to take the plunge. However, I always thought, once I made the decision to publish at all, that someone would pay me to do it. So, paying someone else for help was out of the question.

As I began the process, I realized I had an awful lot of work to do. Forget the manuscript—I had to develop cover art, write introductions, a cover page, dedication, acknowledgments, and a bio. And that's before I even though about formatting for a printed version. The original manuscript had been done as a standard Word doc, which is not an acceptable format.

After playing on the site for a few days, I found that the online tools were not easy to use or intuitive. I had received several phone calls from a sales person for the site I was using trying to sell me very expensive services to help with my efforts. I did continue to try to use the site, but found that it was too difficult. I have to believe that the primary reason for its existence is to sell services. I scrapped the idea and began the tedious process of sending out query letters again. More rejections and more encouragement to self-publish followed. So, I once again took to the Internet in search of the best tool to use.

I eventually settled on CreateSpace. This is a company that is owned by Amazon and that brings several advantages. The first is the ease with which you can post your book on the Amazon site and the professional looking page you get for your efforts. It also offers the ability to post a version for the Kindle, opening the door to e pubs. CreateSpace also has an inside sales team that follows up and offers paid services. The primary difference, in my experience, is that when I politely declined, they proceeded to help me to understand how to proceed on my own. Keep in mind, I did not want to pay one dime to publish, so using online free software and researching through web posts and blogs was critical to accomplishing this task. I have to believe that since this is an Amazon company, their primary goal is to sell books, not additional services, although they can and will if you do not have time or patience to do it all yourself. I don't want to make this sound easy. It took me two months of 8 hour shifts every day to get the manuscript up to standards, develop cover art, re-format the book, etc., to get to a reasonable finished piece.

CreateSpace was a good fit for me, because, although it took some getting used to, once I had the knack of it down, making changes, reposting the manuscript and uploading new versions was fairly straightforward. I did have to rely on other online tools for help. I used Microsoft Publisher to create the book cover using a photo of the painting I took with my iPhone. In order to use it for a cover, however, I had to upload the image to GIMP to give me the pixel concentration I needed. I also used a free version of Adobe Photoshop (free trial).

In short, I was pleased with the results of my efforts and feel that Create Space was the right tool for me. It was easier to get the process started and there was help available.[4]

These two stories are helpful in documenting some of the challenges of print-on-demand platforms. Nevertheless, if you've got something important to say about your passion or mission, print-on-demand platforms may be the way for you to go. Reread Jan's and Ray's stories and use their experiences to vet your options prior to making your final choice.

You can also easily create an eBook for distribution over the Internet or to electronic readers like the Kindle or Nook. Companies such as BookBaby (www.bookbaby.com) and Booktango (www.booktango.com) tell you how to do it all, from design to revision to publishing. You'll also want to be familiar with Smashwords (www.smashwords.com), a free service that enables you to publish to a number of different electronic formats from a Microsoft Word document, charging only a commission when a reader buys your book.

Whichever way you go, it's a good idea to get familiar with publishing law, and I recommend Jonathan Kirsch's *Handbook of Publishing Law*, which provides a wonderful analysis of publishing contracts, tips on avoiding lawsuits, and a number of other important topics.[5]

I implore you to consider making writing and publishing as elements essential to your nonprofit. These would include announcements, calls to action, press releases, thank-you letters, and the occasional grant application. They will bring critically important publicity to your organization and visitors to your website, thereby assisting you in gathering volunteers, sponsors, and funders. And again, if you're not a writer, do make an effort to find a volunteer or someone on your board who is.

CHAPTER 11

Grants, Consultants and Crowdfunding Platforms: Churning and Burning in the Funding Mill

When we first started our nonprofit, we really did attempt to get funding through writing grant applications to large donors. We had big ideas. A theatre-museum with a temperature- and humidity-controlled film vault was our biggest proposed venture. While successful in getting small grants from Arts Council Silicon Valley (now Silicon Valley Creates), a community-funding organization here, we failed just about everywhere else. It wasn't for lack of trying. We read the right books,[1] spent up to twenty-seven hours on each grant application, and were even approached by a consultant who wanted to charge us $35,000 up front to show us how to get Really Big Funding (no guarantees, though). The fact was, we didn't have what a significant number of the grantors in the funding world wanted.[2] We weren't feeding starving children, finding housing for the homeless, or hosting arts events in arenas. But we did have the mission that was purposeful and important, so we came to the conclusion that we were best served doing the good work we did and not worrying too much about Big Ideas in Funding. We geared up, stopped crying, and decided, come hell or high water, that we'd thrive and sustain despite a lack of major financial funders.

Ichigenkins, Rafflesia, and glass insulators probably fall into the same funding situation as the films we were saving, great concepts that held little interest for major funders. So I'd like to tell you about some of our experiences, with the understanding that you just might run into similar situations yourself. And maybe we can save you a bit of time. Others have been there before. You know you'll need to derive much of your support from the community at large, and governmental agencies when possible. As I stated earlier, we've had significant successes with sponsorships to our Keynote Program. This chapter presents a discussion of other means of funding that you'll want to consider, whether or not you actually adopt them (and some you really should). Nonprofit consultants, large funding organizations, pass-through grants, volunteer and individually initiated employer grants, online crowdfunding platforms, people who mean well but want you to do all the work, and being good to funders who are good to you are all topics worth discussing in the fascinating, frustrating, ever-changing world of funding your organization.

A Word About Nonprofit Consultants

Somewhere along the way, you'll either consider or be approached by a consultant who works with nonprofits and he or she will talk to you about how you can be assisted in getting a grant. Consultants, of course, can't guarantee that you'll get a grant. We talked with a couple of them and hired neither. Being underfunded really helped us with those decisions, too. The first one was briefly mentioned earlier. Thirty-five thousand dollars was the entry fee, and he suggested we obtain a seed money grant to pay for that. The thought did occur to us that if we could get $35,000 we wouldn't need a consultant. We did try talking to another organization that helped nonprofits, for a fee, of course. We spoke to the CEO and agreed to meet with one of the organization's consultants. But we had a stipulation. Since the first consultant with whom we spoke didn't really "get" what we did, we told the second group that I wanted to talk with a consultant who had a passion for film, and they agreed to that. We met with the consultant, paid for two hours of the individual's time, and discussed fees and what the individual could do for us. At one point, we suggested that we put the consultant on our e-mail list so we could invite the consultant to our shows and keep that person up to date on our news. The consultant told me not to, as the volume of e-mail was getting to be too much. And this was from the person who allegedly had a passion for film.

We came away from both of these situations with the understanding that we were too small for these consultants to care about and that we were better off doing things on our own. In retrospect, and in further discussions with a few others who are involved in operating small nonprofits, I think we were ahead of the game. Directly or indirectly, nonprofit consultants don't get paid unless you pay them. So if a well-meaning person advises you to talk to a given fee-based nonprofit consultant, agree to do it as long as that individual pays your bill. In one situation, an individual sponsor actually did fund the services of a consultant for us (see Snowden Becker's story in the next section).

Applying for Grants with Really Big Funders: Is It Worth Your Time?

Unless you have a volunteer who just loves to write grant applications, you may very well find that the time you take to craft one will represent a significant loss of your productive time. You might better spend that time elsewhere, including spiffing up your website, writing articles, and doing research. Particularly in the arts, where our nonprofit exists, granting agencies commonly have people with "interesting personalities" who more than occasionally do have power and can grant or deny you on a whim.

Here's a story that underscores this. We were once invited to meet with a huge private foundation by an employee who contacted us and thought we were worthy of a grant. The purpose of the meeting was to determine if a potential grant application would have any chance of passing muster. The employee was not in a power position but liked our work, understood what we were trying to accomplish, and thought we were a good candidate, so put a meeting together. Attending our meeting was an individual who had the power to make something happen or put the kibosh on the whole deal. I took out my notepaper, wrote down the Power Person's name, and since this person didn't give me a business card, I also asked for this individual's title. This is always a good business practice, as you always want to know the responsibilities and pecking order of the people to whom you're speaking. I thought the meeting went well. But when I called back to discuss next steps, the employee told me the Power Person wasn't going to approve any application we submitted. Why? Because I'd had the temerity to ask for that person's title and that question was deemed offensive. We therefore were not invited to pursue the matter further.

Here's another story for you to consider, and you can draw your own conclusions from it as it relates to your own organization. We actually did hire a grant writer, as we had what we thought was a project so important that it absolutely had to be done, and done quickly. It involved filming interviews with older filmmakers who would discuss their careers in academic classroom film. These people were aging and would be gone in a few years. The idea of hiring a grant writer with previous success had been suggested by David Wexler, President of Hollywood Vaults, who had agreed to fund the work of the grant writer. We agreed that Snowden Becker, who had written a number of successful grant applications for film-related projects, would be our writer. We both knew her personally and liked her savvy and professionalism.

Snowden identified approximately thirty potential funders, six of whom she felt were worth applying to. She applied for grants with each of the six. None of them ended up funding any part of the project. In a later postmortem, she discussed the failure of the process with us. One main issue was that our genre, academic classroom films, was of no fundamental interest to the funders, although they had funded other film archives (we were ahead of the bubble, and today our genre holds greater interest in the cinematic world).[3] Another was that as a small organization we were not on their radar screens. A third and final challenge was that they were inundated with grant applications from a large number of applicants. In spite of the fact that they were familiar with Snowden, her applications hadn't been able to cut through the noise.

From a philosophical perspective, Snowden Becker remains an important supporter of the AFA and offers what I think is an important contribution for readers of this book. She suggests that if you're going to go down the grant path, do have an actual conversation with someone at the granting agency first, before submitting your proposal. That individual can make recommendations on how to craft the application. Just as important, he or she, often under the cover of nondisclosure, will tell you if you have a chance of getting a grant. If you're told that you don't, is it worth your time to pursue that path?

Becker also notes that it's the case with a number of funding organizations that first-time applicants seldom get funded, simply part of the "rules of the game" set by those who write the rules. Even a professional grant writer can't break through those ramparts if your organization is small, relatively unknown, or carries a mission that is not perceived as being important to said granting agencies and organizations.[4] Becker goes on to relate:

> Further to that, I'd note that other grant makers ONLY offer funds to a short list of entities that they've already identified as strategic partners— and they don't accept or fund proposals from anyone not already on "the list." One film foundation with which I'm familiar is a good example—they have a small number of "member archives" they work with, and if you're not already at one of them, you can't propose a preservation project to them. In that case, it wouldn't matter how many times you applied, or how worthy your project was, or how closely your work was aligned with their mission—that proposal would just be going into a black hole. You have to get on the list first, and again, that requires a considerable amount of wooing and relationship-building with people who are actually on the inside at the funding source. It's not impossible—but you have to ask if it's a good use of your limited resources, especially if the scope of their giving is likely to be really narrow ... [at] the Center for Home Movies [www.centerforhomemovies.org], we have spent countless hours as a board debating whether it's worth it to pursue grant funding for specific projects, when the proposal process takes so much time and is such a crapshoot. And that's to say nothing of the reporting requirements, some of which are really onerous for a small, all-volunteer organization (quarterly spending reports and budget revisions? Come ON!).[5]

The paperwork requirements to which Becker is referring can be onerous. You will most probably be asked to compile a final report on the use of the grant and may have to file interim reports as well. Some granting organizations contractually require that your organization carry insurance policies for employee theft and personal and general liability. They might even ask you to sign a certificate of insurance, listing their granting organization as an additional insured entity.[6]

The grant situation can be grim for the mid-market 501(c)(3), too, as discussed by Symphony Silicon Valley's President, Andrew Bales:

There are few new groups of any size being created. I am certain there are still a number of ventures started when they serve the founding members' needs (local artists who form a 501(c)(3) to enable them to apply for grants to cover some expenses tax free), but that doesn't mean there are many civic enterprises being created. When a theatre or a symphony or an opera closes, you don't see many of those locations recreating them. We did in San Jose but that was 12 years ago and we were the exception then. Our ballet began life in partnership with Cleveland and when the Cleveland Ballet closed nothing has replaced it there, even after thirteen years. The American Musical Theatre closed in San Jose about 6 years ago and nothing is on the horizon to replace it. I expect there to be a number of other groups that follow the same pattern. Even in our case we are a vital part of the community, but the scale of the former Symphony has not been re-created. We resized to a very different scale. New York City Opera just closed, but before it did, it shrank to a tiny fraction of its previous scale. It is unlikely to ever return or if something does emerge from its ashes it is more likely to be tiny rather than a major civic company.[7]

Bales also noted that midsize nonprofits are being squeezed, from a granting perspective, between very large, well-known nonprofits and small nonprofits. "Even if the smaller ones only take 3 or 4 percent of the pie, the losers are most often mid-size organizations."[8]

Pass-Through Grants

There may be some value in seeking funding from alliances or affiliates that have secured grant funds specifically to redistribute them to other nonprofits. We have secured grants through Silicon Valley Creates (SVC), which has funded our travel to the annual Association of Moving Image Archivists (AMIA) conference, which benefits our organization in a number of ways. Regardless of the focus of your nonprofit, you should make yourself aware of all local organizations making pass-through grants. I mention SVC here because you may very well have a local organization—not always art related, either—that will give you small grants that consist of support given them by local companies that are intended to be passed to local nonprofits. For instance, Applied Materials, a Silicon Valley–based high-tech company, has created a grant program called Applied Materials Excellence in the Arts. Grants are given in the following two areas:

- Technical Assistance awards of up to $2,500 for activities that support administrative development or organizational infrastructure. There are no submission deadlines for Technical Assistance applications. Proposals are accepted and reviewed monthly until May 30.
- Project Support grants of up to $5,000 for exceptional artistic development or programming enhancement opportunities. Project Support proposal deadlines fall quarterly.

The good news for you is that such pass-through grants such as these are specifically intended for smaller nonprofit organizations. Corporate donors to these programs do so for a number of reasons, one of which being that they do want to donate to worthy causes but don't want the overhead of administering the program themselves.

A Flock of Bluebirds: Pass-Through Grants Coming from Over the Transom

In the sales business, a "bluebird" is an unanticipated order that no one knew was coming. It wasn't in the pipeline; it just arrived on its own, sort of flying in through the window. Having a great website is important, and that's how the California Preservation Program found us. They e-mailed us with this subject line: "Don't miss this this opportunity! Funding to preserve your California-related audio, film or video recordings!" And here's part of the text:

> Primary source sound and moving image recordings of the 20th century are seriously endangered by physical deterioration, lack of playback equipment, and rapidly advancing format obsolescence. Time is running out.
>
> The California Preservation Program, through the grant-funded California Audiovisual Preservation Project (CAVPP), has started a web-accessible collection of historic Californiana called California Light and Sound. To date, there are 697 recordings available online from 23 Project partners. Now the CAVPP is reaching out to more California archives and libraries to identify new partners and to preserve more historic Californiana recordings.
>
> Do you have historic, unpublished, recordings of local, regional, or statewide significance? If so, please consider joining the CAVPP! The CAVPP's free services include digitization, metadata management, quality

control and long-term preservation and online access, bringing to light little known recordings via the Internet Archive.

Someone, somewhere will be interested in what your nonprofit is doing and may very well offer you funding or services. These people will be doing web searches. I reemphasize the value of having a keyword-rich website that will increase the odds of their finding you.

Volunteer and Individually Initiated Employer Grants

Your volunteers and other individuals in your sphere of influence may work for companies that have employee-initiated grant money available for local nonprofits. Just ask them. If the companies do, the grants generally come in three forms: employee-matched grants, standard nonprofit grants, and in-kind grants. In the first form, the employee makes a donation to your nonprofit and his or her company matches it. The second form is a standard grant in which the employee fills out a grant request form but isn't required to match the donation amount. In the third case, the company provides something of value to you, which could be hardware, software, or even space. We have received employee-initiated grants from large companies such as Adobe, Applied Materials, and Intuit. Companies like these encourage their employees to support nonprofits as a way to inculcate a culture of philanthropy, so always ask the people who support your mission to inquire whether such a program exists.

To Make Your Grant Application More Successful...

As detailed in a case study in Appendix I of this book, Executive Director Roxanne Valladao of Plumas Arts has achieved a *98 percent success rate* in getting grants through applications. She notes the value of first "doing your homework and investigating" the funding organization before taking the time to write an often time-consuming grant application. She offers these strategies as worthy of consideration:

1. Is the funder public or private? On the one hand, private funders are not subject to the same scrutiny as public-funded entities. They can be more discretionary in who they fund, for what, and how. On the other hand, federal, state, county and municipal funders usually have to be more transparent and accountable to the public that contributes the tax revenue from which their funding is derived.

2. Does the funder have a track record of funding "people like us"? Go to the funder's website and check the criteria for funding to determine if you qualify. Some ideas to consider are:

> Does it fund your type of organization/work, your field of work (arts, education, social service, et cetera)?
>
> Does it fund in your geographic location? Most funders fund in specific cities, counties, or areas of a state or nationally.
>
> Make sure you look at their list of previous fundees. Do any of them appear to be similar to your organization in size, scope (rural or urban), culture, or geography? How about the number of people you serve? Is it a similar number to those organizations that the funder has supported in the past? If the funder's focus seems to be too far from who you are and what you do, it may not be worth your time to submit a grant application.
>
> Ensure that your organization stacks up well against other organizations that will be competing for a given grant. How long have you been operating? What is your reputation within your community and in your area of interest? Do you have impressive people/organizations/entities that will recommend you? Have you gotten a grant before? Are you and your organization well respected in your field?
>
> Are you a good writer? Can you write well enough to get your point across while avoiding grammatical errors?
>
> How competitive is the field? Will the granting organization fund 10 of 150 applications or more like 50 percent or more? Judge the odds. There is much less money now than in the past, and many nonprofits are competing for an increasingly small money pool. It's getting tougher and tougher to get funded.

3. Get on the peer review panel. Some public funding entities (California Arts Council, National Endowment for the Arts [NEA], for exam-

ple) have their grants evaluated by a peer review panel process. If you can qualify as peer or expert in the field of funding, see if you can apply to serve on that panel. You will have to read a lot of grants and it will take a good chunk of your time (usually unpaid). *But* you will learn how some grant applications are more successful than others in terms of clearly explaining what they want to do and how they plan to achieve it. The financial and managerial integrity of the organization is a key focus of any peer review panel. Questions the panel will address include:

- Is it likely that the nonprofit can pull off what it says it will do?
- How well does the application stand up against the others up for consideration?
- Is the grant application complete (was everything submitted that was requested)?
- Did it meet most or all of our funding criteria?

You also get some great ideas from reading all those grants with the added benefit of spending several days with experts in your field. I became a much better grant writer after being on several California Arts Council grant review panels.

4. In advance, communicate with at least one individual at the granting organization. For example, e-mail, call or meet with the public relations person at the funding organization. Talk about what you are proposing to do and determine if the funder is encouraging of your effort or if you both agree that what you want the money for is not what the granting organization wants to fund.

5. So you didn't get funded on the first round? Call the funder and ask why your grant was not funded and how you might improve it in a future application. I have gotten at least two grants on the second try by doing this and reworking the second application.

A Discussion of Online Crowdfunding Programs: What Didn't Work and What Did

In their book *The Networked Nonprofit*, authors Beth Kanter and Allison Fine note that "crowd contributions are 90% useless" but go on to state that "the 10 percent that *is* good is really worth it."[9] That seeming dichotomy reveals the fact that there are very few replicable rules that guarantee crowdfunding. I'm going to discuss one crowdfunding initiative that didn't work and follow it with one that did, so you can make your own judgment.

Back in 2007, we here at the AFA decided that joining an online fund-raising platform group could have some merit, so we set up a crowdfunding account for our Save A Film initiative. It never brought in a dime. That wasn't necessarily the fault of the platform, however. The problem, we believe, is that with thousands of organizations' hands out seeking to feed starving children, cure cancer, and protect endangered species, people who are interested in projects listed on web-based fund-raising platforms aren't much interested in arcane art forms like ours. Historical, cultural, and botanical organizations aren't typically what people are looking for when they go there to make donations. Take a look at the projects being funded on any of those sites and you'll see what I mean. There are at least seven of them as of this writing: CauseVox, Crowdrise, Fundly, GoFundMe, indiegogo, Kickstarter, and Rally.org. They charge between 5.75 percent and 9.5 percent, on the average, to process any donations you might receive. Read the fine print, as you may not be able to collect anything if your project doesn't fully fund (see Don Campau's comments in the next section).

A Crowdfunding Program That Worked

Don Campau is a veteran noncommercial radio executive who's been involved in starting and running radio stations over a career that spans forty years. He's now involved in starting yet another nonprofit radio venture and successfully raised a few thousand dollars recently through a crowdfunding campaign. Here's his story:

> I have been involved in a couple of "crowdfunding" projects started to help fund two community radio stations for which I volunteer. In both cases, we chose indiegogo (www.indiegogo.com). We had heard or read that with one well-known platform, unless you raised your entire campaign goal, your project would receive nothing.[10] We therefore chose indiegogo because you get any funds you have raised (minus the indiegogo percentage). You don't have to make your goal with indiegogo. It's fairly easy to set up and use. Register, and fill in the requested fields

for your project information. In addition to text information you can add pictures, links and even videos to your campaign page.

If your project is under the umbrella of another 501(c)(3), the funds will initially go to that organization, which would forward the funds to your nonprofit. On the other hand, if this is your own 501(c)(3), you will be able to display the tax exempt status so that donors can use this for their own tax records.

The main tool used to make this successful was social media. The larger your volunteer group, the greater the chance you have of spreading the word as well. The basic idea is to first let people know about your new fundraising campaign in some novel and compelling way. People are frankly tired of having hands stuck out at them for dough. They must understand the goal or Mission Statement and "buy in" to your idea. So, you might send out e-mails, make phone calls, blog, tweets and of course Facebook to make your case in a sincere and easy to understand way.[11]

Of course you can also have live events or special presentations that feature your organization where you can distribute your link and information. Drive people to your indiegogo site and keep your other revenue streams going, but do not overshadow your indiegogo campaign. Do not lose focus by spreading your volunteer efforts too thin when you are running a crowdfunding project.

After you make your first announcement, you need to keep at it, every day if necessary and in every social media you can think of. And your volunteers must do the same. The challenging part is to keep your message fresh and offer new perspectives on your project. You can also offer gifts or "perks" for various levels of donations. Some projects have had very interesting and special gift offerings, and this is where you can tap the resources of your volunteer base. Handmade arts and crafts, music CDs, t-shirts, dinners, and even personal appearances can be offered. The sky's the limit on what you offer people without spending too much to get these perks.

One person should be in charge of the whole campaign but it is crucial that your volunteer base create a buzz to everyone they know. But do not brow-beat! There is a fine line between tasteful repetition and over the top "pestering." If people can't contribute, you can simply ask them to share your indiegogo link and help spread the word. An indiegogo campaign usually has a time limit, of say, sixty days (or whatever you choose). You need to keep it as limited as possible to avoid burning out possible donors, yourself and your volunteers. As the time limit nears an end, the urgency to make your goal becomes a motivating factor in your communications about the project. When your program ends, indiegogo will inform you of how much it will take (a small percentage) and then deposit the money into your account.

Make sure you communicate clearly with your donors with personal thank you notes and information about when they will receive their perk (if there is one). In my experience, the more personal you can make this, the more successful you can be. It is important to communicate a human and sincere approach. You will also be able to use the project platform as a database to communicate with your donors, update them, and perhaps, ask them again (after a decent amount of time) to support again.

When it's over, you can assess the value of the campaign. You may want to do another one but pace yourself. You will want to have some kind of grace period before you ask for support again. This has worked for many but it is not a magic pill. It takes hard work, relentless repetition, volunteer effort, patience and a high degree of perseverance. My suggestion is to go to one of your projected funding platform's active campaigns, see how other people are doing it, and then tailor your program based on the talents of your volunteer group.[12]

One thing that we found surprising about this successful crowdfunding project, which took place in a semirural area of Northern California, was that the average age of the volunteers engaging in this program was over forty, an indicator that social media savvy isn't limited to Millennials. As an experiment, you might want to consider launching a crowdfunding project to support exotic flowers, Japanese stringed instruments, or glass insulators. As Campau suggests, you'll need to marshal your volunteers to get their friends involved and you can't stack multiple campaigns in short time frames. Select one individual to lead the campaign. After it's finished, evaluate your results to ensure it was a worthwhile use of your—and your volunteers'—time.

A Note on Well-Meaning People Who Want to Create Additional Work for You Without Doing Anything Themselves

In operating your nonprofit, rarely a month will go by without some well-meaning person offering up a suggestion for fund-raising that involves your time, not theirs. To paraphrase, "Here's what I think you should do to raise money." These suggestions are in the category of "*I'll* supply the idea; *you'll* do the work." "Hey, thanks," you think. "In addition to all the things we do for no pay and little thanks, I'd just love to waste a few more precious hours of my life filling out applications. After all, I've got nothing better to do!" This is endemic in the nonprofit arena, as History San José's Jim Reed relates:

> And of course their "brilliant idea" is something so obvious, or so stupid that you thought of it years ago, or are not demented enough to have ever considered. I had someone say to me: "I just read that Brad Pitt likes history. You should ask him for money." The only healthy response is to back away slowly and then bolt for the exit.

Here's an actual example of one we got recently: "Have you heard (or know anything) about Crowdfunding? If not you should look into it ... it might be a natural way for you to get some small financing in place so your director/producers don't have to write you checks."

This type of thing occurs often enough that I created the following boilerplate, which you're welcome to use:

> Great idea about crowdfunding. Would you look into it and head up the project for us? We're so busy doing everything else here at the archive but love great suggestions on how to raise money, particularly when someone sincerely offers to help (we're all volunteers; why not join us?) Just ask me for our tax ID numbers, and we'll give you all the info you need to set it up for us, thanks.

If you do get any takers, let me know. It will be a first.

Taking the High Road: Be Good to People Who Are Good to You

When you get funding, ethical issues do come into play as to how you spend it. And that means sometimes, when you take the moral high road, you've got to give some of it back. Here's a story that underscores that.

One bright day, we decided we'd be the Johnny Appleseed of 16mm film archives. We'd collect loads of duplicate films, then find people in various cities who, like us, had a passion for 16mm film and would open their own nonprofit archives and provide free shows to the viewing public, exactly like Lorenzo Milam once did with his idea of propagating public radio. Our first candidate was an archive in a large Midwestern city, run by our officer there, Margie Newman. In addition to overseeing the collection and putting together film shows, she started looking for soon-to-be-deaccessioned film collections in her local area. She soon found a film collection owned by the school district in her city. She wanted to save it and found a local funding foundation to give us more than $10,000 to do just that. She and we agreed to house the films, shelve them, curate free local film shows, catalogue them and do what it took to ensure their safety. Margie moved the films to a controlled environment and commenced using the films for free public shows. Within a year or so, the project ran into several glitches. Margie took a new career position in another city. Our new local representative didn't work out as well as we'd hoped. And the storage venue wanted its space back. We had a bunch of films, no one to look over them, and a nasty deadline looming to move the films. Margie found a local nonprofit that agreed to take the films, and they were moved to its location. The new operation agreed to curate shows. And we still had some of that donation left.

I told the new operators that if they needed any assistance on shelving and storage we could help; just let us know when they needed our support. I wanted to see how they fared on their own before disbursing the money, so waited and watched. They never requested anything. But a few months later, they decided they didn't want the films at all. So there we were all over again, trying to find a home for the films. We tried like the dickens and just couldn't find a new home. On their own, the new local operators gave the films away, and we couldn't track the new owner. We didn't know if they were even a nonprofit (by law, the films could only be transferred to another nonprofit). So we threw up our hands and concentrated instead on other elements of our mission. But we never touched that foundation's grant money. It just stayed in the bank, unused.

A short time later, the funding foundation called us to ask about the films. What was the status? So we told them the whole ugly story. We had an idea of who had the films, so we told them where we thought the films might have ended up. We also mentioned that we'd taken a complete inventory, so gave them the list. And we told them their money was safe. We'd used only a portion of the funds. The foundation did its due diligence, found the films, and asked for its money back. Fair enough. I wrote them a note, explaining all we'd done to preserve those films, including inventorying, and said we'd like to be reimbursed for the time we'd spent. I asked them to come up with a figure they thought fair. They came up with an amount, I thought it reasonable, and we agreed to send the amount they wanted back to them. They got our check within a week.

Sometimes you'll secure a grant for a specific project, but even with your best intentions and actions it just won't work out. Don't spend your grantor's money on anything but what it's intended for. Keep it in the bank. Be honest with it. Then, if the you-know-what hits the fan you can be magnanimous and ethical and agree to return the money. If you made an honest attempt to make the project work, the granting organization will, in all probability, want to reimburse you for your efforts. By doing it this way, you will sleep better at night and have taken the ethical high road and perhaps even enhanced the reputation of your organization, even though the project didn't work out the way everyone had hoped.

I mentioned that we returned their money immediately. I do believe that immediacy is important also in thanking donors and funders as quickly as possible after the funds have been received. When we get tax-deductible contributions, donors get an acknowledgment letter from us within a week thanking them and stating their tax benefits.

Wrapping It Up

Funding is an often abstract concept in which logic and virtue aren't necessarily paths to fiscal success. Your funding efforts can and will be stalled by granting organizations that sometimes lack professionalism, people who could be offended by just about anything, and Sincere Folks who offer suggestions of how you could do your fundraising job better but are unwilling to help.

This is why clarity of mission, a "can-do" attitude, and knowledge that you're changing the world—in your own way—to be a better place can provide you with the perseverance to succeed, given your own and important definition of "success." I encourage you to have so many keynote and side projects relating to your nonprofit that you'll always have something fun, interesting, and important to do when a funding initiative crashes. That way, you can concentrate your productive time on doing great things instead of fund-raising.

Be honest, ethical, and fair dealing and you will succeed in your objectives, preserve the reputation of your organization, and—in spite of the glitches—have a great time running a nonprofit that focuses on taking the high road.

CHAPTER 12

Fund-Raising Programs and Techniques That Could Present Problems

As discussed in the last several chapters, there are a number of ways to go about raising money. Some, like Keynote Programs, benefits, and events, I love. Others can be problematic, from the perspective that engaging in them may potentially do your organization more harm than good. In particular, you don't want to offend people who have already donated to you by over-soliciting to the extent that they won't donate again. The Cygnus Donor Survey of June 2012 bears this out. According to the report, "reducing or eliminating support to charities that over-solicit" was among the top two responses to questions relating to how donors are changing their giving philosophies. Charities aren't always listening, either. When donors attempted to voice their concerns, only 25 percent of them were satisfied with the response, while 43 percent noted that none of the not-for-profits reduced the ongoing appeals, even after a complaint was made.[1]

Many of the traditional means that charities have used to solicit funds are now associated, by many people, with scams. The Federal Trade Commission's verbiage on its "Before Giving to a Charity" page says a lot about the perception people have of certain means of solicitation:

> These days, charities and fundraisers (groups that solicit funds on behalf of organizations) use the phone, face-to-face contact, e-mail, the Internet (including social networking sites), and mobile devices to solicit and obtain donations. Naturally, scammers use these same methods to take advantage of your goodwill.[2]

The nonprofit world has been slow in understanding how consumers feel about certain means of fund-raising. There are seven funding areas that represent the most significant potential minefields. They are telemarketing, direct mail, work-related solicitations, neighbor-initiated solicitations, relatives and "past friends" solicitations, planned giving, and borrowing money. Four of them have some merit, if done with a lot of thought, care, and intelligence. Three of them, telemarketing, soliciting from relatives and past friends, and borrowing, are not recommended.

There are some important legal aspects as well. Your fund-raising activity may also require you to register your activities with your state and pay a yearly fee. This is particularly relevant if you engage in mass direct mail, telemarketing, and door-to-door solicitations, as the spirit of this regulation is to prevent fraud. The Unified Registration Statement (URS) represents an effort to consolidate the information and data requirements of all states that require registration of nonprofit organizations performing charitable solicitations within their jurisdictions. It was developed by the National Association of State Charities Officials and the National Association of Attorneys General, an element of the Standardized Reporting Project, with the goal of standardizing compliance under the states' solicitation laws. For more information, visit the URS website at http://www.multistatefiling.org.

What Kinds of Solicitations Can Be Problematic?

First, I'd like to philosophically tackle the issue related to the never-ending appeal. As I mentioned earlier, I think it's important to avoid harassing your donors with seemingly endless appeals for more money. It's a matter of treating them like you'd like to be treated yourself. Initial approaches are important, too, and a good rule of thumb is if you don't like it, why do it to others? All of us in the nonprofit world think our organizations are unique and provide critical benefits. We're out to make the world a better place and want people to join us. We carry a sense of urgency and purpose. As a number of nonprofits have discovered, though, the end doesn't always justify the means. I've made references to several of them that encountered serious legal problems because they didn't subscribe to that concept. But erring in the form of questionable funding practices doesn't always cross the legal barrier. Thinking through how your donors and potential donors perceive your solicitations is what this chapter is all about.

You don't want to insult the intelligence of your donors and don't want them feeling like they've been solicited as carnival marks or village idiots. I emphatically believe you can have a successful nonprofit by treating your donors with respect. For re-emphasis, you'll want them to be treated as you yourself would want to be treated. And solicited.

I've come across a number of funding recommendations in various "how-to" books for nonprofits that I consider to be of dubious value for smaller organizations and offensive when used aggressively by larger nonprofits. In one of those books, the author actually used the example name "Joe Schmoe" in the text to refer to the fictitious name of a donor who had made a contribution. That's not how I'd want to refer to an example of a donor, even as a fictitious one. Especially in a board meeting. Setting a professional tone when internally discussing potential fund-raising operations provides you with a very good baseline from which you can create programs for donors you both love and respect. Always respect your donors.

Let's take a critical look at some fund-raising practices that have traditionally been used by nonprofits, and ask yourself whether they're really right for you. A guerrilla nonprofit is aggressive, radical, and unconventional. Do keep in mind, as you read this, that aggressiveness should be beneficial, not detrimental, to your cause and your approach. If the harassment factor is high with a given fund-raising approach, you will defeat your purpose and achieve an end that will quite possibly leave you worse off.

Telemarketing

The resounding success of the National Do Not Call Registry is an indicator that people do not like solicitation calls. One 2007 survey indicated that 72 percent of Americans had registered on the list.[3] That represents the wishes of millions of people. One aspect of the law is that in many, but not all, states nonprofits are still allowed to make intrastate solicitation calls, provided that they're made by nonprofit volunteers or staff. But that doesn't mean people like getting these calls. If you're thinking of using your volunteers to make such calls, please reconsider. Take an informal poll of your friends and you'll soon discover that most, if not all, of them, consider solicitation phone calls of any type that they receive at their homes to be a form of harassment. You might also found that they've implemented caller ID technology so they can just elect not to answer phone calls coming from people they don't know. It's not fun bothering people and getting rejected, and nothing will burn out a volunteer faster than being involved in an occasional or ongoing boiler room operation.

Direct Mail

The most common uses of direct mail on the part of nonprofits involve renting lists of suspects (sometimes referred to as "prospects") and mailing to a "home" list of people who have already donated or otherwise expressed interest. I'm not a big believer in mass-mailing solicitation campaigns for small nonprofits that rely on rented name lists. The average return rate for mass mailings to rented lists is quite small and continues to decrease as people increasingly throw non- first-class mail in the recycle bin without reading it. They throw away first-class mail as well when it appears to be a solicitation. In addition to the potential costs associated with hiring a direct mail consultant and renting a list, the materials costs are high, considering return envelopes, inserts, and other gizmos a consultant may suggest you include.

You want to be careful of how you manage follow-on mail to people who have already donated to you, because it's not difficult to annoy donors if you constantly ask for money. How? Let's say someone donated $100. You begin sending them monthly $150 "minimum donation" follow-on letters. You photocopy a "handwritten" note in blue on the envelope, saying it's urgent. I'd guess that most of us have received this kind of treatment after we've donated to nonprofits, particularly large ones. From my own experience, there's an organization I used to support and I sent them a decent donation one December. They followed it up for the next two years by sending me mailed solicitations once a month. And therefore I understood the truth of the matter: they'd used my donation to create more than 100 dollars' worth of junk mail to send me over the course of two years. That's how they'd used my money. They'd probably rented my name out to other organizations, too.

Another large nonprofit I supported was even worse. After I'd donated and got an identical junk mail treatment, I finally opened one letter, and guess what? They told me that since I hadn't responded to their urgent mail requests, they were going to telemarket me, so they could tell me "in person" how much they needed my donation. And when I called this organization's headquarters to get my name off their telemarketing list, nobody answered the phone. There was no one to complain to.

I don't like the practice of selling your donor lists to other organizations, either, so the donors can be direct-mailed and telemarketed by others. So what's acceptable? Create a periodical newsletter that provides news about how you're benefiting those who you serve, and you can ask for additional donations there, toward the end of the newsletter. By providing newsworthy information first, you're telling real stories about how their donations are working. Ensure that your mailings are perceived as news, rather than purely as solicitations. For more on crafting a direct mail or e-mail newsletter, see the "Publicity and Publishing: Getting Others to Know About Your Work" chapter.

Work-Related Solicitations

Again, there are good practices and bad practices. The former would be in letting your colleagues know about any charitable causes in which you're involved, perhaps by posting something on a bulletin board in a lunchroom. Asking them directly to support your cause can lead to uncomfortable feelings on both sides when someone doesn't care to contribute. The worst-case scenario involves a manager asking his or her employees to contribute to a charity he or she supports. Not wanting to put a reporting relationship at risk, few people will decline their manager's request, but many will resent it, potentially fueling discord in the workplace.

Neighbor-Initiated Solicitations

A number of nonprofits ask people to visit their neighbors and ask for donations, essentially setting up neighbors to be door-to-door solicitors. This has been done for years by the Girl Scouts and Little League teams selling cookies and candy. Then it evolved to cancer research, starving children, nuclear proliferation, and the homeless. Many have started to dread seeing their neighbors ringing their door-bells, armed with clipboards. Yes, neighbors might occasionally contribute, but again, there's the resentment factor involved with a perceived friendly visit being turned into a request for money, no matter how worthy the cause. But perhaps the biggest contributor to people refusing to answer the door for any reason is the proliferation of scammers, from dodgy repair solicitors to magazine scammers. Here's how the AARP put it in a recent article:

> But the biggest potential danger, especially this time of year, is door-to-door salespeople. Each spring and summer, hired crews of teenagers and young adults canvass neighborhoods inhabited by retirement-age homeowners, falsely claiming they're selling magazines to raise scholarship money or collect for charity. This can not only dupe you into paying up to three times the usual price for magazines that may never actually arrive but can put you at physical risk.[4]

People these days are leery about answering their doors, and many have installed security cameras on their front porches for that reason. Many people won't answer the door for any reason, unless they know in advance that a friend is showing up. Again, one major concern here is volunteer burnout. As with telemarketing, many volunteers come to your organization because they want to help, but that assistance may not mean that they're very enthusiastic about acting as unpaid solicitors.

Relatives and "Past Friends" Solicitations

Want to make a few new enemies and get cut out of a will? One recent book I read suggested "hitting up" (yes, that's the term that was used) grandparents, cousins, and friends the readers hadn't seen recently. I feel that I'm stating the obvious, but grandparents can be very wary of their adult grandkids asking for money, even if it is for a nonprofit cause. Often, grandparents are on a fixed income and, even though they might have money in the bank, you might be resented for asking for some of it. Younger relatives, too, might be extremely resistant of your using family ties as revenue sources. The only possible exception to this that I can think of is if your nonprofit is somehow involved in finding a cure for a physical malady to which your extended family is genetically predisposed. If that's the case, ensure that your nonprofit looks good on Charity Navigator (www.charitynavigator.org) in terms of how it spends its money. You wouldn't want your relatives to feel that instead of donating to a charitable cause, they were paying your salary.

Charity Navigator, incidentally, is a website I highly recommend that you use whenever you decide that you want to donate to a large charitable organization. If the charity in question, for example, spends the lion's share of its finances on fund-raising rather than on supporting its programs, that could be a red flag. Before you donate, please consider doing some due diligence on the organization. And of course, make sure your own nonprofit is squeaky-clean.[5]

In terms of reconnecting with old friends so you can convince them to give you money, let me tell you about an old friend of mine. Every two or three years, she contacts me just to ask for money, usually for a charity that she's currently involved in. Puts me on the e-mail list, too (thanks, just what I need, more spam). That's the only reason that she contacts me. From my perspective, she's gone from being a friend to an acquaintance.

As I said earlier, of course your nonprofit is important. But if your fund-raising ardor damages your relationship with family and good friends, you really might want to reconsider whether you want to continue asking them to fund your charity. My suggestion is that you strongly consider whether you want to do it in the first place.

Planned Giving

I know this flies in the face of what many nonprofits do, but I admit to feeling queasy about having a formal program involved in asking people to remember us in their wills. I don't want our friends and supporters to die, and mentioning their demise seems to me to have a subtext of "please hurry up and die so you can leave us your money." I regularly receive such pronouncements from nonprofits I support. "Remember us in your will," the statement usually goes, found somewhere in the nonprofit's newsletter. I don't like it, and it gives me the heebie-jeebies. A number of other nonprofits also feel that it's a ghoulish way to make a buck. So we don't do it.

Silicon Valley Creates' Grants Manager Audrey Wong disagrees with me on this issue and notes that for some organizations planned giving is crucial to sustainability. She notes the following about how the request is presented: "It needn't be blatant or insensitive ... it could be something as gentle as a sentence on a donor letter acknowledgment page that says 'Please contact our office if you would like to talk to us about a legacy gift.'"[6]

To us, it's again a matter of "taking the high road," although each nonprofit will have its own definition of what that road looks like. I like to work on funding projects that make us all feel good, including sponsorships, Keynote Programs, and the occasional grant that flies through the door. That said, we have been remembered in some of the wills of our recently deceased filmmakers, like Johanna Alemann and Bill Deneen. We promoted their work, sometimes exhaustively, but that's in our mission statement. Their largesse came as a surprise, welcomed but not solicited.

Borrowing Money

There are certain financial situations that should be warning flags to you. One book on nonprofits states that "borrowing to make ends meet" may be an option for cash shortfalls and suggests borrowing from board members, local foundations, or even taking out a small business loan.[7] If you are challenged financially to the extent that you need a loan, your nonprofit is probably in peril. Instead of borrowing, you may want to consider some severe paring, which might include having a frank discussion with any paid employees you might have and asking them to convert to full-time volunteer status. None of them will be overjoyed at this prospect, but you'll have credibility if you, as the director, do it first and lead the way. Another worthwhile idea is to look at your office expenses. If you're paying rent, maybe it's time to look at in-kind donations for free office space or shared services (see the "Setting Up Your Sustainable Nonprofit Office" chapter for this and more money-saving office ideas). If your financial situation is grim, you might also seriously consider whether you should merge with another nonprofit or have that organization absorb your operation into theirs. If those options seem viable, author Jane Arsenault, in her book *Forging Nonprofit Alliances*, offers some suggestions as to important issues you'll want to consider as you investigate these potential solutions.[8]

It all goes back to the initial planning you and your team did when you originally put your nonprofit together. If you decided that paid employees and rental space would be your modus operandi from the beginning, did you also discuss contingency plans for sustainability if the coffers dried up? Going backwards can impact morale, and merging operations can result in outcomes that may not be in accordance with the original vision, mission, and objectives of your nonprofit.

CHAPTER 13

The Cutting Edge:
Thinking Outside the Box

As you build your mission statement and website, create your Keynote Program, hold events, and publish newsletters, you'll continually encounter new ideas, some of which you and your team come up with, others of which are generated by those you serve. Many of these notions may, when addressed or enabled, expand the horizon of your nonprofit corporation in terms of the number of people you reach and serve. As your scope becomes more encompassing, you'll write about it, which will drive additional visitors to your website. And they may end up becoming supporters, even though they may not live in your locality. Again, keywords and SEO (search engine optimization) techniques draw people, and much of that will come virally, through Internet searches. Since your goal is to ensure that at least one-third of your funding comes from contributions, membership fees, and gross receipts from activities related to your organization's exempt functions (see "The First Step: Forming Your Nonprofit Corporation"), you'll want to come up with interesting new ways to serve and engage your public, locally, nationally, and internationally, which will assist you in coming up with additional public-funding sources.

I encourage you to stretch the envelope as you consider other things that somehow, someway, can be logically linked to what you do. Here are several examples of how "thinking out of the box" has helped our nonprofit in several different ways. They're all related to film, of course, but please consider the overall creative approach we used and apply it to your own nonprofit.

The public performance initiative of us here at the AFA was, initially, in doing film shows at no charge. One filmmaker, Bill Deneen,

140

lent us a copy of his film *The Happy City* (http://archive.org/details/happy_city), filmed in 1956 in a Burmese Hansen's disease (leprosy) colony high in the mountains. Several decades after it was filmed, I was in Burma on a trip and decided on a whim to visit the city of Kyaing Tong to see if the hospital was still there. It was, I met the nurses and the residents and wrote a short piece about my visit, which I then added to the film notes I put on our website. This began a long, rewarding relationship with Deneen, who became one of our biggest benefactors. He encouraged others to sponsor films for uploading to our Internet site, and soon other filmmakers joined in. Wherever you travel, make an attempt to visit someone or something that has a relationship to what your nonprofit is doing. Introduce yourself and discuss your mission and how you're going about accomplishing it. Make sure your business card has a link to your website and do consider having your mission statement printed on the reverse. You'll meet allies and affiliates and perhaps even discover a new funding source.

Being "cutting-edge" means that you take the extra effort to make discoveries and bring them to your audience, perhaps in nontraditional ways. You can break new ground. I discovered *morlam* music from Thailand while on a trip there, bought a bunch of video CDs and created a show that we did several times in the United States. We wrote the film notes, added them to our website, and now, if you type "morlam music" into Google, we're in the top ten. How did this fit within our mission? We've always shown lots of ethnographic film, and this represented a cultural experience on Video CD, a format rarely sold in the United States except in markets catering to ethnicities from other countries. A large part of our mission is to save films from being destroyed, and we were concerned that videos in this format might be going away as well. From our perspective, it fit.

In another case, I was enchanted by a film we showed about the *haenyeo* divers of Korea, women who dove for seafood and kelp without the aid of breathing apparatus. I took a vacation one year to the island of Jeju-do, briefly met some of the divers, who are now very old, went to the haenyeo museum, and bought a book there. That trip led us to put up the old film on the Internet (http://archive.org/details/Korea 1975) and I'm happy we did, as this may be the last generation that performs this arduous job and up to now this is perhaps the only film—

to my knowledge—distributed in North America that discussed the lives of these women.

How does this apply to you? Be focused on your mission, but always be ready to expand your scope to include new ideas that will augment your work and programs. Your ichigenkin nonprofit should make connections with both stringed instrument and Japanese-American communities wherever you travel. You might later get invited to do a show there that will be sponsored, and you may be able to pick up subscribers to your nonprofit as well. And in further study on ichigenkins, you may realize a commonality with other Asian stringed instruments little known in the western world. I encourage you to keep an open mind, as one of the threads you follow could end up dramatically increasing your service area, audience, and sponsorships.

If your Rafflesia nonprofit involves housing exotic plants, you may be able to be listed on a horticultural tour. Dozens of publications, from daily newspapers to magazines, may be interested enough to do a story when it blooms. Your focus on Rafflesia may lead you to add other parasitic flowering plants to your programs, events, and writings. You might even expand to more exotic plants of Southeast Asia.

Your telephone pole insulators share something with computer chips, don't they? Silica is used in making both glass and silicon chips. Insulators were an essential part of electrical and telegraph transmission and were essential in railroad signaling. You therefore have a plethora of technology communities, museums, and publications that you can consider for alliances or as affiliates or publicity partners. Your website can link to them, and it can be reciprocal a significant percentage of the time.

You Can't Always Go "Public"

Occasionally, there may be a worthwhile project in which you'll engage but you can't write about, just yet. But you can talk about it. In our holdings, we have a very old film made in an African country with a significant nomadic population. In this particular country, this population was ejected from ancestral lands as the nation formed a new national park. We were contacted by representatives of the nomadic group, who told us that they might be able to secure repatriation relief if various individuals could prove that the land in question was ancestral. To prove this, these individuals would have to recognize ancestors in the film located in geographical areas identified in the shots. A representative of this group would be willing to take the film around in a jeep and show it to the individuals in question. If positive identification occurred, the information would be used in a court of law. We copied the film in a format that could be shown in the field, took the film to Africa, and presented it to a representative ourselves. Why couldn't we go public with this? Because the nomadic representative was also a government official and going public would have possibly put that individual in danger. This was a "cutting-edge" project that, while providing no current publicly reported benefit, had tremendous future value. And it provided contemporary relevance to an old film that we had saved. Eventually, once the court case has been resolved, we hope to make the story public.

As you can see from the previous examples, your imagination is the only limit to your creativity. I encourage you to adopt a "why not?" philosophy in terms of broadening the horizons of your nonprofit. In particular, listen to your volunteers and sponsors. Sometimes their wild ideas, you'll discover, aren't so kooky after all.

Political Correctness, Revisionist History, Religious Dogma, and Other "Mind-Traps"

Be wary of anyone telling you what you should or should not do based on prevailing thought, current scholarship, popular discourse, or religious dogma. "Out-of-the-box" thinking encourages everything from brainstorming on anything under the sun to just plain crazy ideas. If your organization is going to do public presentations, I can guarantee that at one time or another you'll get someone angry about something. You do have to play fair, too. I read the liner notes to a record album of aboriginal songs, with a caveat to ensure that the record not be played where aboriginals could hear it, because it might provoke ghosts. Does that mean you don't play it on the radio, where aboriginals could be in the listening audience? If you make your decision based on indigenous religious practices, will you also give the same consideration to the Catholic, LDS, and Scientology churches?

Lorenzo Milam's KTAO-FM in Los Gatos, California, used to routinely play programming from the National Socialist White People's Party, a Nazi group.[1] There was never an on-air caveat, either. The tapes just rolled. People got angry. Lorenzo called it "good radio." He wanted people discussing the material. History is in a constant state or revision. Ambrose Bierce once wrote that "God alone knows the future, but only an historian can alter the past." I recommend that you keep a very open mind about how history—as it is currently written—affects the output of your organization.

One example that we encountered at the AFA comes immediately to mind. In terms of film programming, our policy has been to show everything, regardless of who thinks a given film shouldn't be shown. Sometimes we buck the scholars. Years ago, a film called *Cave People of the Philippines* was deaccessioned from a significant number of film libraries in the United States. Its veracity was sullied when it was reported that the protagonist of the documentary film, Manuel Elizalde, had faked the story about a "stone-age" ethnic group he had allegedly discovered. Our archive has one of the comparatively few surviving prints of this film.[2] We knew that during the time the film was made Ferdinand Marcos was legally purloining traditional lands in order to profit from timber licensing and sales. We showed the film, positing that perhaps Elizalde was engaged in a crusade to assist the Tasaday in securing their land from encroachment and had promoted them publicly as a way of achieving that outcome. By re-contexting the film, we found great value in showing it. Today, scholars seem to be continually revisiting Elizalde's relationship with the Tasaday. Politics and political correctness blow with the wind, so we've always believed that avoiding either represents a policy that we can live with, now and in the future.

In dealing with politics and political correctness, try to think through the larger issues. In 1993, the San Jose Museum of Art mounted an exhibition featuring a number of local Vietnamese-American artists. One of the art works featured the image of Ho Chi Minh. Conservative factions within San Jose's Vietnamese community—the largest in any city outside of Vietnam—threatened the museum with violent protests, and museum management responded by canceling the exhibition. As an alternative, they might have chosen instead to run the exhibit anyway and add a teaching element regarding Freedom of Speech and the Bill of Rights.[3]

Your own community may very well have special interest groups that don't believe that anyone with opinions differing from theirs deserves a right to be heard. I fundamentally do not like censorship, but others love it. If you'll be doing anything, exhibit-wise, that could offend any group in your community, it's worthwhile to think ahead of how you'll deal with a protest, including managing public relations and your relationship with the press and law enforcement.

Overall, I'd suggest that you think about the value of having an open mind-set on any public program you might wish to stage and even perhaps establishing a non-censorship policy as part of your operating procedures.

Creating an "Out-of-the-Box" Approach

As we've seen, there are a number of things you can come up with that represent "thinking out of the box." As a publicly funded charity, you've got to come up with ways of reaching new people, to feed the educative mission of your nonprofit and to get additional donors, sponsors, and perhaps grants as well.

I can't emphasize enough the value of "touch." I've always felt that the essence of the nonprofit world was, in a sense, the celebration of "people." I think you'll agree, too. Even if your nonprofit is geared toward the investigation and elevation of a passionate subject, if lots of others can't enjoy it with you it's not as much fun. The people you touch may be anonymous to you. You might have interacted with them once or twice. Or it may develop into a relationship where you're in constant communication. Sometimes, you'll reach people in a way that you'd never dreamed. As I mentioned earlier, I personally don't like to discuss having our nonprofit included in someone's will. I've got a professional and ethical problem with it, although it seems, at times, as though I'm in the minority on that subject. Ten years ago, we worked with a filmmaker to put up a web page on our site with a picture, bio, and filmography. She was in her nineties, and no one from the film world had been in touch with her in quite some time. I only talked with her twice. I was saddened last year to hear that she'd passed away and shocked that she'd left our nonprofit quite a bit of money, by our standards. I was told that our connection with her had made a positive impact on her final years. I never knew.

At our nonprofit, our volunteers are constantly thinking of great and helpful things we can do for people. We like to do nice things for filmmakers, like putting up pages that highlight their careers on our website and assisting them in uploading their films so people can see them, sometimes for the first time in decades. We want our visitors to see the films free of charge, and in making this possible, light up everyone's life a bit: the filmmakers, our visitors, and us, as well. To me, that's the ultimate reward in making a nonprofit successful. It takes some, money, for sure, but a lot less than you may think. So think out of the box, touch a lot of people, and make as many of them as happy as you can, as an element of your mission.

CHAPTER 14

Keeping the
Government Happy

While some view the Internal Revenue Service as an adversary, I look at it differently. I relate to the IRS as a valuable partner that facilitates tax-deductible financial transactions so that a competent, honest nonprofit can fulfill its mission. It's actually quite simple. The IRS has made operating a 501(c)(3) nonprofit corporation a great way to promote your area of expertise, and although you do have to make an effort to raise funds from the public, you can, as this book attests, run a nonprofit on very little money. This chapter covers some simple basics but is not to be considered as a substitute for legal counsel or professional tax advice. It should, however, enable board officers, staff, and volunteers to carry on informed discussions with these professional advisors. It's always a good rule to consult a tax expert or attorney should a question arise.

You do have to ensure that you file your reports on time, pay your taxes (see below), document your annual meeting, adhere to your bylaws, and act within the provisions of the nonprofit regulations. You need to have some of your documents ready for public inspection. You also want to make sure that your donors of $75 or more receive letters breaking down the value of any goods and services they receive in return. Where some nonprofits run into trouble, though, are in areas such as failing to observe the general rule against self-dealing, getting too heavily enmeshed in the political arena, and making a surfeit of money from activities not directly related to the mission of the nonprofit.

Here's what the IRS says about those issues in the Article 8, IRC 501(c)(3) Tax Exemption Provisions:

Section 1. Limitations on Activities

No substantial part of the activities of this corporation shall be the carrying on of propaganda, or otherwise attempting to influence legislation [except as otherwise provided by Section 501(h) of the Internal Revenue Code], and this corporation shall not participate in, or intervene in (including the publishing or distribution of statements), any political campaign on behalf of, or in opposition to, any candidate for public office.

Notwithstanding any other provisions of these Bylaws, this corporation shall not carry on any activities not permitted to be carried on (a) by a corporation exempt from federal income tax under Section 501(c)(3) of the Internal Revenue Code, or (b) by a corporation, contributions to which are deductible under Section 170(c)(2) of the Internal Revenue Code.

Section 2. Prohibition Against Private Inurement

No part of the net earnings of this corporation shall inure to the benefit of, or be distributable to, its members, directors or trustees, officers, or other private persons, except that the corporation shall be authorized and empowered to pay reasonable compensation for services rendered and to make payments and distributions in furtherance of the purposes of this corporation.

The reference to "Bylaws" under section 1 means that you included this terminology in the standard boilerplate from which you crafted your bylaws. In addition, you probably agreed to this in the Articles of Incorporation you originally filed with your secretary of state.

The Rule Against Private Inurement (Self-Dealing)

You, as the director, are allowed to be salaried. So are your officers and employees. But salaries must be "reasonable" and in line with what others in the same capacity make in similar organizations. Salaries cannot include a percentage of profits or other "private benefits," including transactions involving anything in which an individual associated with the organization has a material self-interest.

A famous case relating to this was the situation involving the United Way's onetime CEO William Aramony. When he was accused of self-enrichment, an internal audit could find nothing to substantiate it but did find that his travel expenses hadn't been vetted properly and documentation was incomplete in terms of separating business expenses from personal charges. After several newspaper articles were written, the IRS and FBI conducted separate investigations. In 1992, he and two others were indicted, charged with defrauding the United Way of $1.2 million. He was convicted of a number of charges in 1995 and was sentenced to eighty-four months in prison.[1] The United Way received more than a black eye. Public trust in the organization was severely eroded and several United Way affiliates left the organization and changed their names.

Some well-known self-dealing issues have occurred in higher education as well. In the early 1980s, Tufts University professor William Douglas was alleged to have embezzled tens of thousands of dollars in grant money, giving a significant amount of it to a "working girl" as a paid researcher who did little, if any, research. The lurid case eventually involved the murder of the woman, Robin Benedict, as documented in Teresa Carpenter's book *Missing Beauty*.[2]

The undermining of faith in public charities is a big factor in the popularity of Charity Navigator (http://www.charitynavigator.org), a watchdog website that allows potential donors to see what percentage of their contributions will be spent on budget areas such as administration and fund-raising, versus programs and services. Charity Navigator was further discussed in the "Fund-Raising Programs and Techniques That Could Present Problems" chapter.

Avoiding Politics

501(c)(3) nonprofits are prohibited from involvement in political campaigns for or against a given candidate and are severely limited in terms of acting to influence legislation. If you intend to engage in any activity in these areas, it would be advisable to consult an attorney well versed in nonprofit law to ensure that by doing so you're not jeopardizing your status as a charitable organization.

Even when you're not in violation of an IRS regulation, just the appearance of having a political agenda can harm your organization, particularly where donations are concerned. In 2012, the Susan G. Komen for the Cure organization found itself in the center of controversy, as a result initially funding, then rescinding its support for a program run by Planned Parenthood. The controversy was sparked by abortion rights issues, and in the wake of the political melee an estimated 15 to 30 percent of participants in Komen's fund-raising efforts dropped that year.[3] Soon thereafter, Komen's CEO and VP of Public Policy both resigned.

It is therefore strongly recommended that you, as a 501(c)(3) nonprofit, be self-critical in steering clear of any notion of political advocacy or affiliation.

Deriving Revenue from Unrelated Activities

Your representatives at the IRS take a dim view of nonprofits that make too much money from activities unrelated to their core missions. It makes sense. If you start making truckloads of cash from a commercial venture, you've become a for-profit company and are supposed to be taxed as such.

So what's legal, from a nonprofit perspective? Let's say you decide to sell ichigenkins in a small shop inside your museum. It doesn't represent a significant percentage of your yearly revenue, but it does "promote" public interest in that instrument, if that's part of your mission. But now you decide to manufacture ichigenkins. You sell them all over the world and derive a significant income from them, as they're sold in many venues other than your own. The income is well more than you obtain from grants and public donations. Chances are that the IRS would view these two before-and-after scenarios in a different light.

Or say you open a nursery to sell Rafflesia but begin to add succulents. Then soon you add bags of soil additives, then grass seed, rolls of sod, and lawn mowers and sprinkler systems. You hire two employees to install lawns and sprinkler systems, and pretty soon you have a landscaping business that greatly outstrips the income you derive from grants and donations from the public. That acceleration of non-charity-related income may very well pique the interest of the tax authorities.[4]

There are gray areas, to be sure. In the case of us here at the AFA, it has been suggested that we offer footage copied from a number of the films in our archive and license it on the open market. Aside from the expenses relating to the equipment we'd have to buy to make this happen technologically, we're not positive that this activity would fall under our mission "to acquire, preserve, document, and promote academic film by providing an archive, resource, and forum for continuing scholarly advancement and public exhibition." If we did it and made a significant amount of money from that business, I think there's a good possibility that the IRS might consider us a footage house and not a 501(c)(3) public charity. For more on this topic, read IRS Publication 598, *Tax on Unrelated Business Income of Exempt Organizations* (http://www.irs.gov/pub/irs-pdf/p598.pdf).

Your Annual Meeting

Every year, you'll have your annual meeting, the minutes of which will be added to your corporate records book. Your Secretary will, in most cases, record the minutes. It's a good idea to schedule the meeting six to eight weeks in advance. People's schedules change from year to year, so your original preferred date may have to be modified, and advance notice gives everyone an opportunity to ensure the date is available. I recontact everyone again a week before our meeting to remind them.

To conduct the meeting, we use a modified *Robert's Rules of Order* mechanism, where we first address last year's minutes, then have a director's and CFO's report, followed by discussions for any new business.

The director's report is important, as it logs all the significant activities in which your organization has engaged during the previous year. For that reason, I start collecting data for my next year's director's report immediately after the previous year's meeting. Every time something important or exciting occurs, it goes into the revised director's report that I'll deliver at year-end. That way I don't forget anything, because I'm constantly adding material as the year evolves. The day after the meeting, I e-mail my report to our Secretary so it can be added to the minutes of the meeting, and the Secretary can add any officers' comments to it easily. Same thing for the CFO's report. When the

Secretary returns the completed minutes by e-mail, everything is compiled and put in our corporate records book.

It's our objective to have our annual meeting last no longer than one and a half hours. We make our annual meeting into a staff event and include our volunteers as well as our officers. After the meeting, we all go out to a good but inexpensive restaurant. We do this for two reasons. One is that we want to thank everyone for what they've accomplished that year. The other is that away from the formal meeting there's lots of brainstorming. Over dinner, it's common for topics that had engendered no discussion at the formal meeting to be brought up again and discussed, after the team has had a chance to think about them. New ideas are created and discussed as well at dinner. Many of the new thoughts that were initially suggested over dinner and drinks were discussed, argued, finessed, refined, and later implemented. This combination of formal meeting followed by an informal round-table has served us well over the years. People are serious about keeping to the time frame of the formal meeting but do have time to suggest new ideas and comment on them. Afterward, the informal time allows for numerous discussions and brainstorming and the only time limit in effect is the one imposed by the closing of the restaurant. We do give the restaurant a heads-up on the number of us that will be there so we can get our own table or our own room. We have a fun, passionate, and boisterous team, so we like to be courteous toward other diners by sitting apart from them.

Your Annual Tax Return

Being an underfunded nonprofit organization has one huge benefit, in terms of paperwork, over more robust nonprofits. Most tax-exempt organizations are required to file an annual tax return with the IRS, although certain church-affiliated organizations and governmental organizations are not required to file. Tax law, of course, is always subject to revision, but here's a digest of the information regarding annual tax documents found on the IRS website at http://www.irs.gov/Charities-&-Non-Profits/Form-990-Series-Which-Forms-Do-Exempt-Organizations-File%3F-(Filing-Phase-In):

- If your gross receipts are normally greater than or equal to $200,000 or if your total assets are greater than or equal to $500,000, you'll have to file IRS Form 990.
- If gross receipts are under $200,000 and total assets are under $500,000, you may file either Form 990 or Form 990-EZ.
- If your gross receipts are normally less than or equal to $50,000, you'll probably have to file Form 990-N.
- But (from http://www.irs.gov/Charities-&-Non-Profits/Exempt-Organizations-Annual-Reporting-Requirements-Overview-Annual-Return-Filing-Exceptions) "Organizations whose annual gross receipts are normally less than $25,000 are not required to file an annual return, but may be required to file an annual electronic notice—e-Postcard—beginning in 2008."

As an underfunded nonprofit, therefore, if you normally accrue less than $25,000 annually you may have to file only one document, the e-Postcard.[5]

A Note About Sarbanes-Oxley and Its Impact on Nonprofits

The Sarbanes-Oxley Act was passed into law in 2002 and deals with issues relating to corporate governance. Two of the items contained in that law that do have importance for nonprofits are provisions relating to retaliation against whistle-blowers and destruction of documents that could be used in an official investigation. There are also elements relating to audits that are worth noting. The best perspective I've read on its real-world impact to nonprofits was written by Rick Cohen of the *Nonprofit Quarterly*, and appeared in the December 30, 2012, issue, in an article titled "Sarbanes-Oxley: Ten Years Later" (http://nonprofitquarterly.org/governancevoice/21563-sarbanes-oxley-ten-years-later.html).

Documents Available for Public Inspection

You will have to make certain documents available for public inspection during regular business hours at your principal office or at any of your offices that have three or more employees. The IRS imposes a $20 penalty for each day that you don't allow public access and a fine of $5,000 if the obfuscation was found to be willful. The fine is imposed on the person who denied access and not on the organization itself. If requests for these documents are made by mail, you have thirty days to respond and you may charge for copying costs. To view the regulations pertaining to public inspection and penalties, read IRS Document 557, pages 19–21 (http://www.irs.gov/pub/irs-pdf/p557.pdf).

Documents that the public may inspect are:

- Federal Form 1023 tax exemption application, as well as any documents that were attached to it
- Tax exemption determination letter
- Your last three annual information returns (typically, Forms 990, 990-EZ, 990-BL, 990-PF, 990-T, or 1065, with any amendments, schedules, attachments, and supporting documents)

Because they were easy to upload, we've made it a point to have our tax determination letter and bylaws (which we included in our 1023 application) always available for inspection on our website.

Letting Your Donors Know What Is— and Isn't—Tax Deductible

IRS Publication 1771, *Charitable Contributions—Substantiation and Disclosure Requirements* (http://www.irs.gov/pub/irs-pdf/p1771.pdf), describes the breadth of the law in terms of your responsibilities to donors and the IRS. Here are a few of its highlights, in terms of what it means for smaller nonprofits. By law, you have to send a letter to each donor who contributes more than $75 and receives goods and services in return. The letter must contain two elements. The first is a statement saying that the donor can only deduct the difference between the amount of the contribution and the value of the good or service. The second is your estimation of the fair-market value of the good(s) or service(s) the donor receives as a result of the contribution. You don't have to calculate the amount of the tax deduction, but we like to do it for our donors anyway. For example, in our Keynote Program people sponsor the uploading and digitization of films. In return for sponsoring a 400-foot film for $110, he or she would be sent a DVD of the sponsored film, which we estimate to have a fair-market value of $5. Therefore, the donor would be eligible for a $105 tax deduction. As I mentioned in the "Sponsorships: Building a Definitive, Self-Sustaining, Permanent and Exciting Keynote Program" chapter, we always make it a point to mail tax deduction confirmation letters to sponsors within a week of receiving their donations and I add a small Post-it note to the donation letter, too, just to make it a little more personal.

There are also elements specific to larger donations that are worth reading, so downloading and reading IRS Publication 1771 is recommended.

Aside from cash donations, you will probably be receiving donations of goods as well, and you'll need to determine their fair-market value as part of the process of creating a tax benefit letter that you'll send to your donors. For more information on deriving fair-market value, read IRS Publication 561, *Determining the Value of Donated Property* (http://www.irs.gov/pub/irs-pdf/p561.pdf).

Sales Tax

If your organization will be selling goods, you may be subject to your state's sales tax. For more information, you can click on your state's link through the IRS State Link site at http://www.irs.gov/Charities-&-Non-Profits/State-Links.

If You Need a Lawyer

If you're a smaller nonprofit, you may find that one day you'll need the services of a lawyer but find that you have a challenge in paying legal fees. Author Peri H. Pakroo, J.D., has some excellent advice for obtaining pro bono (free) legal assistance. Her suggestions include calling large law firms to ask if they offer pro bono assistance to nonprofits (many of them do) and contacting law schools to ask if they offer free or low-cost assistance by students under the guidance of a law professor, as part of a community law clinic initiative.[6] If yours is an arts nonprofit, you may be able to avail yourself of the services of Volunteer Lawyers for the Arts (http://www.vlany.org/legalservices/vladirectory. php).

Moving Forward

Staying legal is critical to sustainability. But sustainability also means doing your best to ensure that your organization succeeds well into the future, the subject of the next chapter.

CHAPTER 15

Crafting a Succession Plan: Leaving a Legacy and Documenting Your Assets

Eventually, the directorship of your successful nonprofit organization will change. If you don't want to run the risk that the great work that has been done by your organization will be discontinued, a succession plan must be in place. This will provide documentary access and assistance to the people who have agreed to administer the plan. The time to start putting a succession plan together is when you're writing your bylaws, and the process of changing of directors should be included in them. If you're already incorporated but haven't yet put together a comprehensive succession plan to include people, access, and assets data, you can now craft it and present it at your next meeting. By "access," I refer to items such as where your software and Internet applications are physically located, how they're accessed, and what the usernames and passwords are. "Assets" encompass everything the organization owns, from physical collections, to equipment, to computer-related material, and possibly more. Using the checklist in Appendix II at the end of this book, you can begin a list or build on the one you've already created.

Here at the AFA, we didn't actually think of the word "succession" until our first annual meeting, when one of our officers brought it up. At that meeting our VP agreed to be in charge of any eventual succession process, and at the appropriate time would convene a meeting of officers, who would then choose a new director from those currently serving on the Board of Officers. We now have a formal Succession Officer in place as well as agreement from other officers that they will lend assistance should that situation come to pass.

Good planning involves preparing for outcomes that aren't always predictable but do happen. If you're the director, let's get it out in the open and discuss that most dreaded of terms, "your death," projecting forward into the future at such a time that although you're still the director, you're no longer able or available to lead your organization. When you pass on, you're going to go in one of two ways: you'll know either that you're dying beforehand or you won't. In the latter case, you won't even have time to be surprised. This is a real emergency situation, and the world is full of emergencies.

That said, there's also the issue of where all the physical assets of your organization are, what bank account(s) you have, to whom and how your organization pays bills, and the location of databases and other office software. What about your website? Who hosts it? How do you renew your URL? What's the e-mail program? And how about usernames and passwords for everything? What about the password for your office alarm?

It should be obvious by now that you've got to create an access and inventory document that will detail everything. Take a moment to review and complete the checklist in Appendix II. Once it's created, place a copy into your corporate records book and every time you update anything in that document reprint and swap it out for the old one. You also want to give a hard copy to your Succession Officer, if you have one. If you don't, there's a lot of value in creating that position. Do remember, also, to embed the "location" of the succession document within your computer's file structure inside the document itself, so it can be updated by your successors. In MS Word, for example, you can insert a field in the footer of the document that will list the entire file name (Insert>Quick Parts>Field>FileName). Be sure to click the small box that adds the path to your file name. By doing this, you ensure the field listing the file name will change automatically if you ever move the document to another spot in your computer and will be printed on the document itself. And speaking of file names and paths, when you're using software resident on your computer be sure to list in your succession document exactly where, on your computer, your data files reside. That way, if your successors ever need to find and electronically update the actual data files it will be easy for them to find the files.

The aim of this book is to provide ideas that you can implement that will allow your organization to succeed and be sustainable even though you may be underfunded. But nonprofits do fold, particularly when unfavorable financial situations become insurmountable. If you do go out of business, merge, or become absorbed into another organization, you'll still want to document your assets and conduct a postmortem, which should include an analysis of how well you succeeded in fulfilling the objectives of your mission.

If Your Organization Folds

Nonprofits do go out of business, and when they do, they often have to find homes for various assets they hold. As a 501(c)(3) charitable organization, you'll have to roll those assets over to another tax-exempt organization or governmental agency.

Here's the rule verbatim, from Article 8, IRC 501(c)(3) Tax Exemption Provisions, section 3: Dedication and Distribution of Assets (www.irs.gov/publications/p557/ch03.html#en_US_2013_publink1000200064):

> Assets of an organization must be permanently dedicated to an exempt purpose. This means that should an organization dissolve, its assets must be distributed for an exempt purpose described in this chapter, or to the Federal Government or to a state or local government for a public purpose.

The dissolution of your nonprofit may be voluntary or involuntary. If voluntary, you'll have to file Articles of Dissolution with your secretary of state and you may also have to file a tax clearance from your state as well. Dissolution becomes involuntary when taxes have not been paid or annual reports have not been filed. In this case, your state will initiate the proceedings.

There are certain financial situations that should be warning flags to you. As was discussed in the "Fund-Raising Programs and Techniques That Could Present Problems" chapter, "borrowing to make ends meet" is one of them. To reiterate, if you are challenged financially to the extent that you need a loan, the sustainability of your nonprofit may be in peril. Instead of borrowing, you may want to consider some severe paring, which, as I stated earlier, might include having a frank discussion with any paid employees you might have and asking them to convert to full-time volunteer status. You may have to investigate the possibility of not paying office rent and seeking an in-kind donation of space instead. Finally, you might also seriously consider whether you should merge with another nonprofit or have that organization absorb your operation into theirs.[1] If all fails, dissolution of your nonprofit may be your only viable choice.

If you do dissolve, please consider calling several other local non-profits to see if they'd like to have your hardware and software. When we were just starting up, our friends at the Palo Alto French Film Festival were dissolving their organization and gave us software that proved valuable and necessary. There will always be a local nonprofit that will be thankful to receive your donation.

Part of a good continuance plan includes investigating the possibility of rolling your nonprofit organization into another one. While perhaps not as specific as yours as to subject matter, there could very well be other nonprofits doing similar work. It might be worth having some preliminary "what if" discussions with the principals of such organizations. Earlier, in the "Working the Big Room: Building Alliances and Affiliates" chapter, I discussed the value of linking up with other organizations to form affiliate relationships.

Here at the AFA, for example, we have a strong relationship with the Internet Archive (www.archive.org). They host the films we've digitized and uploaded, pay for the bandwidth and storage necessary to allow people to see them, and make it easy for us to complete the metadata for each film. Most important, they understand what we're trying to accomplish and facilitate our mission to make films available for free public viewing. Our organization is a strong one, and we still have much work to accomplish that the Internet Archive won't do, as it's not in their charter. But the Internet Archive and the Library of Congress are just two organizations that could be potential homes for our archived films, and we've developed important relationships there.

Developing relationships with principals at organizations with similar goals and that serve similar groups of people is important enough that I've included a "Potential Successor Organizations" element in the assets checklist in Appendix II. It's important to consider as many possible outcomes as you can when mulling over how your organization will continue to succeed and thrive when you're no longer around to provide direction and motivation. Providing your successors with the names of organizations that could be potential homes for your nonprofit in the future helps to assure that your expertise will not be lost if they ever have to consider making a move in such a direction.

Documenting Your Assets

Assets tend to accrue remarkably quickly, so I'd suggest documenting them from Day One. They may not all be located in one place, either. Here at the AFA, we try to obtain as many Bell & Howell 2592 16mm film projectors as we can, as they're the best we've found for reviewing films. We've temporarily placed many of them with volunteers who review films for us, so we need to keep track of them. There's also a maintenance issue. Only one person repairs them locally. And when a worm gear gives up the ghost, it's not financially feasible to repair them. It's predictable that you'll have your own repair and maintenance situations, so do record into your assets inventory sheet the names, contact information, service rendered, and typical costs associated with that repair vendor.

Again, try to imagine your successors running your organization in your absence, and predict every situation they could run into, any questions they might want to ask you, and any resources you are privy to. Again, a sample access and assets inventory checklist is included in Appendix II. Obviously, yours will differ somewhat, but you can easily build off mine and adjust it to the particulars of your nonprofit. As a final note, it's common for a nonprofit organization to have multiple computers in different locations, so be sure to indicate which software programs reside in each of them.

Wrapping It Up: Conducting
Your Postmortem

The main focus of this book is about putting together a world-class, sustainable nonprofit organization and making it run successfully on a very small amount of money. It's not about how to end your non-profit's life. But if you're working with a really arcane subject, your successors may not be able to adequately continue the successes of your nonprofit. This is particularly the case if they have major time constraints that prevent them from putting in the time necessary to make the organization viable. In addition, some nonprofits have found themselves to be in a situation where their officers and volunteers were at an advanced age and the organization had not been successful in attracting younger officers and volunteers.

If your successors do decide to formally end the life of the organization, that doesn't mean it was necessarily unsuccessful, though. It may well have succeeded in its mission and fulfilled many, if not all, of its goals and objectives. In Chapter 1, "Redefining 'Success,'" I listed the elements of our own mission statement and noted how we were doing in terms of fulfilling our objectives. This should be an iterative process and done continually throughout the life of your nonprofit as well. If you're busy fulfilling your objectives and you're taking all the right measures to be sustainable, I'll bet you're not doing a postmortem at the moment. But when you're creating your succession document, you should also be re-evaluating how well you're succeeding, based on the ways you're using to measure success.

Introducing the Access and Assets Inventory Checklist

I have included an assets and inventory checklist in Appendix II. I encourage you to copy and print it, then begin filling it out. This checklist should be viewed as an emergency master document that will allow your successor(s) to run your operation in the untimely event of your death. There are other emergencies that could occur that could necessitate a succession plan as well. You could be called out of state for an indeterminate amount of time to care for a sick relative or be stranded overseas during a disaster or insurrection. Consider your checklist a turnkey to all of your operations. It should include everything from your alarm and banking information, to hardware and software, to phone and Internet information, repair and supply resources, collections management, and even an entry for potential successor information. Your list may differ or evolve from this one, and I encourage you to be comprehensive. As soon as you've made your first pass, I'd suggest you convene a meeting and ask your officers if anything has been left out. As soon as your document has been completed, file a copy with your corporate information book, then e-mail it to at least one officer.

This document is also intended to be your disaster recovery data sheet. It's also a record you'll keep for insurance purposes (in addition, do consider taking photos or video of your office setup). In California we have earthquakes, in Louisiana floods, on the Eastern Seaboard blizzards and hurricanes. A fire can occur anywhere, at any time. Those tech support phone numbers are important. This emphasizes the importance of either hardware or web backup for all electronic data concerning your operation. If you use hardware backup drives, store them in a location away from your main facility. By backing up on the Internet, as apart from the hard drive on your office computer, you minimize your exposure due to natural disasters. Since this document contains banking and security information, it is important that your Internet security be kept up to date. And always be aware of the danger of getting hacked and having your documents stolen by electronic theft.

CHAPTER 16

Small Is Beautiful: Keeping It Pertinent, Creative, Successful, Sustainable and Manageable

You're starting small but will have dreams. Those imaginings will take you to some great places through projects and initiatives that will be valuable elements in completing the objectives of your mission. If your dreams are big enough, they may carry you to extremes that are grand or grandiose, so monumental that they'll succeed spectacularly or crash wildly. The latter may be for the ultimate good, because you tried, learned from the experience, and perhaps later will succeed because you don't make the same mistake twice.

Learning from failures is actually one of the beauties of doing things yourself. You can read all the books in the world, but until you try it yourself you won't be completely sure if the advice you're getting from them does or does not work in your situation. This chapter sums up many of the points in this book that are essential for small nonprofits to keep in mind.

Win Through Failure: Learn from the Challenges and False Starts

I want to tell you about our own aspirations and how they evolved, why we tried them and how we failed. Through failure, though, we actually made our nonprofit organization stronger. This is a fitting chapter to close this book, because every successful small nonprofit should always be attempting new things and behind every success are a few snafus that ironically contributed mightily to the things that ultimately worked.

As I related earlier, initially we at the AFA were doing public shows in a speakeasy under the streets of San Jose, but we thought that expanding into a formal space that we controlled would allow us to better serve our audience, both through the ongoing shows we originated and also as a venue for traveling cinematic shows. These nearly always bypassed San Jose, the tenth-largest city in the United States. Such shows traditionally skipped our city as they traveled between San Francisco, 60 miles to the north, and Los Angeles, 350 miles to the south. The San Jose Redevelopment Agency was in the process of designating an arts and culture area on South First Street in San Jose and was making buildings available at reduced rental rates. Basically, our idea was to grow the AFA by having an office, theatre, and climate-controlled archival space in this "arts zone," thereby having a permanent "storefront" presence in our city's core. We met with the redevelopment director of the city, but there was clearly no interest in what we were doing and it was made clear to us that no assistance in any form would be made available to us. But that didn't stop our dream.

Margie Newman, our Corporate Liaison Officer, who lived in and did AFA shows in St. Louis, had been networking with a number of high-level political and cultural people in that city. She invited us to consider moving there. The story was compelling. She had gotten us an appointment to visit with the mayor, who had a deep interest in reviving the core of the city. Margie had identified two buildings that would be great for housing us. One was available to purchase for $100,000, a pittance in San Francisco Bay Area terms, and one of our officers had even expressed an interest in buying it, then leasing it to us. So two of our officers and I flew to St. Louis. We met the mayor and some other civic and cultural leaders, saw the buildings, and even looked at housing options. One issue that came up in meetings was the number of people we intended to hire. This would be a ground floor opportunity and we were going to have to build up a grassroots organization anew, so we were frank with them. There wouldn't be a significant number of paid employees when we started. St. Louis quickly lost interest, and we recognized the peril of moving 1,500 miles away to a brand-new city in which Margie was our only initial ally.

Seeing the value in staying closer to home, we then investigated Oakland, California, forty miles up the road. Similarly, they were developing their inner-city plan. Again, funding and employment were two issues that presented a challenge. In the meantime, we had received feelers from two individuals in San Jose who wanted to keep us there. Pat Curia, a preservation enthusiast, was trying to find an organization to take over the abandoned Christian Science church in St. James Park. At one time it had been converted to a cinema and the property was now owned by the city. It was a glorious Greek Revival structure. Again, we struck out. The city had a grand plan to convert it to another use.[1]

Finally, David Crosson, the director of History San José (HSJ), our local history museum, came up with a plan. David had several years earlier invited us to house our collection at HSJ's collection center, we took him up on the offer, and our collection was housed there. San Jose was building a brand-new library, which meant that the old Martin Luther King Library was no longer going to be used. David made a proposal to the city to turn the old library into a downtown history museum and had us occupying a street front corner of the building for our office and archive, and the library had a screening room as well. But the city nixed his plan (the library eventually became part of the McEnery Convention Center).

Re-Evaluating and Reinventing

And thus, after four attempts at seeking to enlarge our mission in three different cities, it made sense to sit back, discuss, and re-evaluate who we were and what we were trying to accomplish. We had to look at the situation creatively. We wanted to better serve the public, but major funding, the rental or purchase of a building, and the overhead associated with having employees would not in themselves accomplish our mission. They might, instead, derail it, if funding sources dried up. Sustainability was a major concern, so we asked ourselves if hitching our wagon to funding agencies was a smart thing to do. Even if we were fully funded originally, what would happen if operating funds were rescinded in poor economic times? So our officers and I made the decision to serve the public instead as a virtual organization that emphasized Internet resources instead of focusing on building our future as a brick-and-mortar operation. By doing so, we felt we could better control our future and mitigate the risks associated with having to rely on major funders or the winds of political change.[2]

Thinking Big by Thinking Small

In essence, our organization was reborn. It took a stone-cold look in the mirror and led to an honest realization of who we were, rather than what we thought we could be. Our mission statement was rock solid, and we could do it all on a shoestring, with lots of help from our volunteers and officers, donated archival space from History San José (whose new director, Alida Bray, understood and appreciated our mission as much as David Crosson did), and the Internet Archive, which gave us the ability to make our films available to millions, instead of a few hundred. In thinking big, toward expanding our audience to the millions, we had to think Small, in terms of our brick-and-mortar footprint. Our new focus retained our pertinence while allowing us to manage our finances toward sustainability and succeed in our mission, the main elements of which were to preserve films and provide public access to as many people as we could. This was a radically different approach for us, and unconventional for an organization that had always thought of the "public exhibition" theme in our mission statement to equate to "theatrical presentation." It was, when it came down to it, the essence of how a guerrilla nonprofit has to operate: self-sustaining, creative, cutting-edge, and yes, underfunded. And, perhaps, being underfunded was our salvation.

And this whole story, I think, represents an encapsulated version of what you might anticipate happening with your organization as well. You don't have to do things big, but you have to do them well. Using your mission statement as a guide, you can creatively make it work regardless of funding issues or civic politics. The fact that your world and the technology encompassing it are in a constant state of evolution is to your benefit. There are continually better ways to do things and more effective ways to reach your audience. Creativity in thinking will produce sustainability as you, your officers and volunteers strive to constantly reinvent and evolve the organization.

That's the reason, as I read more and more about how large non-profits are suffering through funding challenges, that I strongly feel that small nonprofits will continue to have greater importance and via-bility in our changing world. Underfunded nonprofit organizations have the flexibility to move fast, without the baggage of large numbers of employees, out-of-control operating costs, and the insecurities endemic in relying on public and private grants. They can rely on spon-sorships for intelligent, ever-evolving Keynote Programs that resonate with those individuals and affiliates that are aligned with the organi-zation's mission, as carried out by a core of dedicated volunteers. They define the concept of sustainability by creating alliances that can create success through in-kind donations of materials and space.

Much of the advice you'll read in books about nonprofits recom-mends spending significant sums of money. On employees and insur-ance, consultants and facilitators, on office equipment and information technology, on paying rent for a space, on maintaining a website and advertising. And fund-raising costs. For a small existing nonprofit or a start-up, these budget items can put you in the poorhouse. In most cases, you can avoid them through creatively thinking out of the box. You shouldn't even be "in the box" in the first place. When a spending issue comes up, be rigorous in demanding proof that you really do need to spend money, rather than "rolling your own" and doing it yourself. Lean and mean keeps you solvent and sustainable.

Self-reliance is an old-fashioned concept. This book has put it in a shiny new wrapper. In terms of much of the nonprofit world, unfor-tunately, it's anathema. But its time has come, once again, and it's worth keeping in mind every time an issue regarding spending money arises. Smaller, agile nonprofits that rely on themselves, their intelligence, per-severance, and volunteers are the wave of the future in the world of charitable public corporations. Appendix I showcases three organiza-tions of different sizes, structures, and missions that have done just that. This book has shown you how to make it happen, sustainably, efficiently, and successfully. Now you've just got to go ahead and do it.

Appendix I:
Case Studies of Three Lean, Successful and Sustainable Nonprofits

A number of small-to-midsize nonprofit organizations are using the techniques described in this book to further their missions successfully and sustainably. I polled several such organizations in an effort to get their stories of what they did that worked and didn't work, what they learned from their experiences, and what they'd recommend to others. The criteria I used to determine who might be included in these case studies included being a 501(c)(3) nonprofit organization and having been in operation for ten years at minimum. I began the process by sending a questionnaire of twenty-one questions, covering topics ranging from how—if at all—they managed to support their office functions to how they raised money, worked with volunteers, and handled relationships with both nonprofit and for-profit affiliates. The three that were selected are exemplary and their stories and recommendations have much to offer to the nonprofit community.

Jenny Do's Friends of Hue, Roxanne Valladao's Plumas Arts and Craig Diserens's Village Harvest provided what I think were the most valuable case study contributions. Their missions are radically different. Do's focus is international in scope, supporting an underserved community of orphans and economically disadvantaged people. Valladao's organization drives the arts scene in one of California's smallest counties. Diserens's group takes food grown from backyard trees and feeds the indigent. What these organizations have in common is an emphasis on sustainability that has been bred from creativity in terms of how they've dealt with the challenges associated with maintaining nonprofits successfully and meeting the objectives of their missions in the always-uncertain world of nonprofit funding. Whether you're involved in starting a nonprofit or wanting to improve the way your existing organization forges ahead toward sustainability, you'll benefit by reading their stories. Chances are that the challenges they faced will resonate with you and the ways they dealt with these issues will provide some new and worthy ideas that you can apply as well.

Case Study A: Friends of Hue Foundation, Humanitarian Aid to Children in Vietnam (http://www.friendsofhue.org)

The Friends of Hue Foundation (FHF) was incorporated in April of 2000 as a 501(c)(3) charitable, nonprofit tax-exempt, nongovernmental organization (NGO/INGO). The foundation's primary mission is to provide assistance to impoverished people and victims of natural disasters in the Thuà Thiên-Hué Province of Central Vietnam. All staff and board members of the Friends of Hué Foundation in the United States serve as unpaid volunteers. Originally, it was created to address the social issues arising in the aftermath of natural disaster in Hue, Vietnam, such as housing children who had lost their parents during the storms or helping families who had suffered great losses on the same occasions. As is the case with many nonprofits, its mission eventually expanded to address needs of children seriously abused or victimized by human trafficking or other causes, and families suffering from social or economic crises.

While Friends of Hue serves the population of Central Vietnam, its fund-raising is centered in San Jose, California, a city of approximately one million people, an estimated 10 percent of whom are of Vietnamese ethnicity.

As Chairwoman of the board Jenny Do notes, "Our mission is to provide long-term assistance in economic self-sufficiency, health care, education and emergency relief for victims of natural disasters in Thuà Thiên-Hué and nearby areas in Central Vietnam. The assistance projects are diverse, efficient, and flexible in order to accommodate changing needs over time. We operate with approximately ten volunteers here in the United States, including all board members and officers. We have twelve paid employees in Vietnam and none in the U.S. We have no rented office in the United States; we simply use board members' homes or offices for meetings and gatherings. For our work in Vietnam, we have built two buildings in the city of Hué. The land is owned by the local government, but the buildings are owned by the Friends of Hue Foundation. The original board members fund-raised for the first building and the second building was a joint venture with East Meets West, another NGO working in Vietnam."

The bare-bones approach to operating costs in the United States serves to ensure that all funds are spent directly on its mission in Hué. A common question asked of Do is why focus on the lesser-known Hué, rather than the larger population centers of Ho Chi Minh City (Saigon) and Hanoi? "Hué is Vietnam's de facto 'third capital' due to its history and geographical location," says Do. "However, due to its rugged terrain and inhospitable climate, Hué has not been seen as an ideal place for large-scale manufacturing and aggressive economic development. This has resulted in fewer economic opportunities for its inhabitants, many of whom live in poverty. Hanoi to the north and Saigon to the south are both political and economic capitals, respectively, and have received the bulk of attention from NGOs/INGOs, whereas Hué falls short in this respect. Currently, FHF is the only officially registered U.S.-based INGO with a physical presence in the Thuà Thiên-Hué Province."

The challenge of raising funds in an economically inopportune area such as Central Vietnam is addressed by doing the lion's share of the fund-raising in San Jose, primarily through the yearly Ao Dai Festival (www.aodaifestival.org). "We bring together many artists, from designers to musicians, in order to create a grand community event," says Do. "This benefits both communities. We help to provide cultural experiences for the young Vietnamese-American and American community here in the Bay Area while raising funds for the children in Central Hué."

Friends of Hue networks with a number of other organizations, both nonprofit and for-profit, broadening its reach in both the United

States and Vietnam. As Do notes: "We collaborate with many organizations domestically and internationally. For instance, our mobile clinics are done in conjunction with other medical organizations in the U.S. as well as in Vietnam. In the framework of our youth leadership program, several San Francisco Bay Area high school student clubs, as well as Boy Scouts and students from France and other countries, organize youth leadership exchange sessions every summer. We also operate a social entrepreneurship program in order to raise one-third of the monthly budget. Called the Virtual Assistance Center, or VAC, it employs our graduates—children that we raised and have graduated from university—who process all POs and invoices for e2f translations, Inc., a well-established corporation headquartered in California. Our children are paid higher than the local rate. Their earnings for part-time work are more than what our local staff would earn full-time. For every dollar the VAC bills the corporation for its service, the company matches with a donation to the children's shelter. This initiative helps to employ our children in a high-paying job using twenty-first-century job skills (computer skills, English, and Internet-savvy experiences) while helping raise the shelter's children."

Jenny Do adds that the biggest financial challenge has been the inability to obtain large grants for raising abused children. But Friends of Hue remains successful and sustainable through its traditional annual fund-raising and monthly social entrepreneur program. And it has accomplished much, including

- providing free health-care check-ups and medicines to 2,100 patients in Phu An Commune, Thuy Thanh commune and Phu Binh Quarter of Hué City;
- making emergency cash donations to 159 households in Phu An commune, which had been seriously affected by the great 1999 flood;
- providing small interest-free loans to 25 poor households in Phu Hau Quarter;
- building, staffing, and maintaining a shelter for orphans and disadvantaged children in Hué City; and
- providing scholarships to students in poverty who could not afford further educational pursuits.

She has several strong suggestions for other nonprofits wishing to be successful and sustainable: "Don't commit to something that you cannot see through. Factor in human issues for long-term operational success. Volunteerism has its limitations. In order for you to count on your volunteers, make sure the interests of your organization and the volunteers' are aligned. You must consider having a social entrepreneurship program, as relying purely on fund-raising or grants is not sufficient and sustainable."

Case Study B: Plumas Arts, Bringing Art and Culture to One of California's Smallest Counties (http://www.plumasarts.org)

How does an arts nonprofit thrive in a remote county with fewer than 20,000 residents, a 12 percent unemployment rate, and located in a town with fewer than 5,000 people? Ask Roxanne Valladao, Executive Director of Plumas Arts (Plumas County Arts Commission). She's been making it happen there successfully and sustainably for 28 years.

Located in the county seat, Quincy, Plumas Arts serves a small county that straddles the Sierra Nevada mountains in Northeast California. Its office, art gallery, and theatre have a prominent presence on Quincy's Main Street, maintained by Valladao, her three part-time employees, and numerous volunteers. Plumas Arts' story is a fascinating one, and Valladao insists that any small nonprofit can be as successful as hers by replicating some of the sustainability techniques that Plumas Arts has developed and honed over more than two decades.

The Plumas County Arts Commission, commonly known as Plumas Arts, was incorporated in 1981 as a 501(c)(3). Plumas Arts cultivates communities in which arts and culture flourish. As Valladao states, "It develops, designs, and integrates arts, cultural, and educational programs into the life of our county to build quality of life and better human beings. It promotes cross-cultural understanding and assists in community and economic development and tourism." There are seven to 10 people on the Board of Directors, and two locations, the Plumas Arts Gallery and the Town Hall Theatre, both of which are owned by Plumas Arts. "Both are historic buildings that we keep vibrant for the community with ongoing programming. We also produce events in a variety of venues around the county. Our gallery was purchased at a foreclosure auction. We liquidated a 25-year-old accumulated cash reserve to pay for it. It was renovated with community donations of cash and labor. The process was documented in a California Arts Council publication (http://www.plumasarts.org/pdf/art works.pdf). After several decades of managing the Town Hall Theatre movie business and spending the last 10 years building trust in the community, title for the theatre was transferred to Plumas Arts from the oldest nonprofit membership organization in the county, since our mission to keep the facility open for community use was directly aligned with theirs."

In terms of the funding mix, Valladao adds: "Employing a diversified funding base in an annual budget, these percentage usually apply: earned income 30 percent, memberships/donations 15 to 20 percent, contracts for services 10 percent, fund-raisers 30 percent, grants 15 to 20 percent. We have maximized opportunities over the last three decades. This is probably where we gain our greatest traction for sustainability. We employ a diversity of sources, including

- "earned-income programs/projects: movie business, performing arts facility and office rentals, art gallery/ gift shop;
- "fund-raising events: Taste of Plumas (county-restaurant and wine tasting), Mountain Harvest Festival (microbrew tasting), auctions, benefit concerts and the occasional prize drawing;
- "donations and annual memberships: for general support and program specific;
- "fees for services: we coordinate an art education programs in our schools, sell ad sales in our newsletter and art and literary calendar, and we serve as fiscal receivers for compatible arts and cultural groups;
- "California Arts Council (CAC): we have been considered a model local arts agency by the CAC for at least two decades. I have served as a peer review panelist for several grant programs and have been contracted as a consultant for them to help other rural arts agencies. We have gotten annual funding for operating support as the Plumas County representative to

the State-Local Partnership program since our inception (http://www.cac.ca.gov/programs/slpp.php). We also regularly get funding from the CAC through their Artist in the Schools program (http://www.cac.ca.gov/programs/ais.php);

- "in the last two years we have also been funded through the Creating Places of Vitality program (http://www.cac.ca.gov/programs/cpv.php) and we were just one of 24 entities in the state to be funded for the inaugural Creative California Communities program for a "Plumas Artisan Made" branding and marketing training project for local creatives (http://www.cac.ca.gov/programs/ccc.php);
- "county funding: when our county has funding available, they often give it to us; and
- "grant writing: over the years we have been funded by the James Irvine Foundation, CA State Department of Education, National Endowment for the Arts and the Common Good, High Sierra Music and Bill Graham Foundations among others.

"Grants are definitely not the answer to sustainability, but we cannot discount them as a funding source. They are time-consuming to write and there is no guarantee that you will get funded. I have been writing grants for long enough that I do not apply unless we stand a good chance of getting it. I have a 98 percent success rate of getting grants funded for this reason. We also do not make up an application just to match what a funding source is funding. We write grants for programs that are inherent to our mission."[1]

Valladao strongly emphasizes the value of having a diversified mix of funding sources, citing one of Plumas Arts' most significant historical funding challenges: "In 2000, most of our funding came from the California Arts Council. When they were virtually defunded with a 99 percent reduction we lost almost half of our organizational funding. We then went to our membership and asked then to increase their annual donations, which they did. We increased fund-raising events by 300 percent and we took a leap of faith with a nearly bankrupted movie business, bringing it back to life, and making it an earned-income program that has provided funding for most all of the last eleven years."

Plumas Arts is currently undergoing perhaps its most challenging funding dilemma ever. Its Town Hall Theatre is the only movie theatre in the county, and its film show revenue keeps the theatre open for the live performances that Plumas Arts produces and supports. Film distributors will soon only offer films on digital media, and without the estimated $80,000 to buy and install a new digital projector the theatre will not survive. That has prompted a new Keynote Program, the Save Our Theatre initiative. So Valladao is at it again, with fund-raising events that include bake sales, open mic nights, and an online four-minute video that has created both interest and funding (http://www.plumasarts. org/events/helpsavetht.html). Within four months after beginning the Keynote Program, Plumas Arts had raised more than $40,000 in a grass-roots campaign aimed at a county of only 20,000 people.

What's her secret on remaining sustainable? "Keeping a diversity of funding sources and constantly innovating new ones. We seek opportunities or create them. We work well with others. We are creative, resourceful, tenacious, resilient and determined. We have also earned the respect of the communities and constituents that we serve. Those that support us never doubt our integrity and know that they are making a good investment in us. So think entrepreneurially. Be true to your mission. Know whom you serve. Do not pander to any particular funder, but do ensure that you fulfill the contractual requirements of those that fund and support you. And every few years, have your board really ask the question of whether the organization still needs to exist. Change with the times and rise to the occasion."

As an added note, Plumas Arts has made it a point to contribute business-oriented marketing efforts in its ongoing attempt to receive county funding. It's heavily driven by the concept of using "push" marketing with the county to tell of Plumas Arts' "pull" marketing programs and is included here as a template that can be used by any nonprofit arts organization that finds itself having to make a case to a local political body.

Top 10 Reasons for the Plumas County Board of Supervisors to Fund Plumas Arts

10. Even though Plumas Arts is a nonprofit, we serve the function of a commission—without the financial burden to the county of formal com-

missions—with your annual designation for us to serve Plumas in the California Arts Council's (CAC) State-Local Partnership.

9. Plumas Arts is a leader in the state arts agency field, holding nearly legendary status as a model in the rural arts agency. Our Executive Director is contracted by the CAC to serve as a consultant to rural agencies.

8. Plumas Arts provides more programs, services and events than many other organizations combined. For instance:

- Arts Education in all schools K–6 through grant funding we obtain from the CAC, the Plumas County Office of Education and schools match.
- Events ... Words & Music (Open Mic Night), Gallery Openings, and many of the county's premier events, such as the Almanor Art Show, the Mountain Harvest Festival, Taste of Plumas, the Courthouse Art Show and world-class concerts and community performances.
- A first-rate Art Gallery that represents more than 60 local visual artists, providing them with supplemental financial support.
- A Cultural Events Calendar that lists all county cultural events, year round.
- Movies 4 days a week. Plays and performances average another 2 days a week of community use.

7. Plumas Arts programs (make you money) generates revenue for the county with:

- Land & business taxes on the Town Hall Theatre & Capitol Arts Gallery.
- Sales taxes on gallery sales and concessions.
- Employees & payment to artists who pay income taxes.
- Transient Occupancy Taxes—Cultural Tourists spend more money.
- Restaurants and other businesses benefit from increased revenues around our events

6. Plumas Arts operates highly-trafficked community facilities at no expense to the county. We're just like the fairgrounds, the recreation district, and museums, who *do* get annual county funding.

5. Plumas Arts works well with others ... building partnerships with groups of a diverse nature to leverage more for our local communities in grant funding, attendance and private support.

4. Plumas Arts has developed an ambitious and diverse funding base: private, public, earned income, grants, donations, memberships, and fundraising events. We are driven by Passion & Purpose fueled by Persistence. We operate entrepreneurially and support the entrepreneurial efforts of others.

3. Plumas Arts has a good track record of obtaining grants that bring new money into the county and sharing funds with others ($25K in the

last two years helps fund Celtic Fest, Portola City Lights, Farmer's Market Concerts, Indian Valley Mural artist Lacy J. Dalton, Sierra Buttes Trail Daze). We also act as an umbrella for other groups, including Feather River Fine Arts Guild, drama and school arts education organizations: Association of Concerned Theatre-goers, A Few Brews & A Banjo, and Tale Spinners, so they can do the work they want to do without having to gain nonprofit status.

2. Plumas Arts has one of the largest most diversified membership bases in the county.

1. Plumas Arts helps make Plumas County a place people want to live in, move to, raise their family in, and visit, so that they can wish they were one of us lucky folks who live here. We contribute mightily to Quality of Life.

Case Study C: Village Harvest, Delivering Food from Backyard Trees to the Hungry (http://www.villageharvest.org)

How do you solve the dilemma of thousands of tons of fruit being thrown away in a county with a significant number of economically disadvantaged people who don't have enough to eat? That was the question addressed by Joni Ohta Diserens when she started Village Harvest in 2001. Village Harvest is a nonprofit volunteer organization in the greater San Francisco Bay Area that harvests fruit from backyards and small orchards, then passes it along to local food agencies to feed the hungry. It also provides education on fruit tree care, harvesting, and food preservation.

The numbers are staggering. In 2013 alone, Village Harvest volunteers picked 245,000 pounds of fresh fruit, producing 650,000 servings of healthy food for tens of thousands in the community. Founded in 2001, this 501(c)(3) nonprofit has harvested 1.7 million pounds of fruit, which it distributes to those in need through twenty food agencies located in Santa Clara, San Mateo, and Yolo counties.

Its mission is to bring together neighbors and community organizations to provide food for the hungry, preserve local agricultural heritage and skills, and promote sustainable use of urban resources. As Executive Director and co-founder Craig Diserens states, "Village Harvest began based on values rather than a specific cause or need: making good use of gardens and volunteer talent to benefit the community. It started with picking backyard fruit for the 4H to make preserves. But we quickly learned that millions of pounds of fruit were going to waste in our area and concentrated our efforts on reducing local hunger with healthy local food."

This lean, sustainable, and thriving organization has no physical office space and is a "virtual organization" with volunteer leaders and the small staff working from home offices. Much like for-profit Silicon Valley companies, Village Harvest uses computer systems, networks, and telecommunications to work together across a wide area and at different times each individual has available. It operates with three employees, carved up into one full-time Executive Director and two part-time quarter-time staff members. Diserens continues: "Most of our 13 years has been as an almost-purely volunteer organization with limited part-time staff support. However, as we've become much larger and more active it's been important to build a permanent paid staff to provide continuity, expertise, and enough guaranteed resources week in and week out. Village Harvest is still very much a volunteer-powered organization; the role of the paid staff is to maintain the central infrastructure, administration, and funding needed to support all-volunteer community harvest teams all over the Bay Area."

Village Harvest now has more than 1,200 unique volunteers participating each year, with a core of 30 volunteer leaders and 150 to 200 frequent volunteers. Volunteer activities include picking fruit, much of it from backyard fruit trees, and hauling it to storage facilities. Village Harvest has eight community harvest teams operating within four counties in the greater San Francisco Bay Area.

In term of physical assets, Village Harvest rents two storage units in the San Jose area for equipment storage. Its Davis, California, volunteer team has an equipment storage shed the organization owns that is placed on City of Davis land at no charge. It owns one large van, used to carry harvesting equipment such as ladders, that will carry more than one ton of fruit.

Partnerships make operations more sustainable. "We have close relationships with food agencies, and with several we store equipment in their facilities, drive their vans, have access to their buildings, and have harvest teams which begin and end at their facilities," says Diserens. "We provide as much as forty thousand pounds of fruit annually to each of those agencies. We focus on the front of the cycle, and they handle the distribution to people in need. This cooperative sharing of nonprofit resources is key to our lean operating model."

Raising money has always involved grassroots programs, including creatively utilizing material that others might consider to be "garbage." Diserens notes: "In the first few years our primary funding model was to make and sell specialty gourmet fruit preserves, often made from extra-ripe fruit that was too soft to go to food banks but exceptionally sweet for preserves. This was sufficient to raise five to ten thousand dollars per year for equipment and basic expenses, enough to cover all our expenses in the early years."

"As we grew, we began to ask homeowners and volunteers for financial support. We encourage, but do not require, homeowners that we provide harvesting services to make a donation to cover a portion of our costs of providing our service. We do one annual fundraising appeal in December. We do not currently solicit funds from individuals outside our base of homeowners and volunteers."

Village Harvest has established an effective way of obtaining funds from for-profit companies as well. "We draw upon the employee support and matching gift programs of major corporations," says Diserens, "which provides much-needed funds, and also gives us visibility and recognition inside those companies."

As the organization grows and matures, Village Harvest is expanding its funding sources. "Village Harvest has not solicited grants for most of our history, although some small foundations discovered us and we won national awards of two- to three-thousand-dollar grants," says Diserens. "In 2011 and 2012 we began a transition to a paid staff model to sustain the organization long term. The evolution from an almost pure volunteer organization to a small paid staff has major financial implications. Given the need for dramatically more funds, we began applying very selectively to local foundations for grants, starting small in the two- to ten-thousand-dollar range. This resulted in a small number of grants each year, and we have a one hundred percent success rate so far, largely the combination of our track record and targeting grants that were good fits. We have been able to grow the size of our grant requests to fifty thousand dollars now that we have proven ourselves with those funders."

A major focus of Village Harvest at the present time is continuing on the path to sustainability, as Diserens and the team are evolving the organization to handle the ever-growing needs of its service community. "Sustainability is so much more than money," he notes. "It's people, values and mission, know-how, relationships, funding, and thinking ahead through the future of the organization. Village Harvest is in a multiyear transition from our origins as an all-volunteer, founder-driven organization to a truly sustainable organization that does not rely on the know-how or volunteer service of the founders and has sufficient staff and funding to maintain programs indefinitely. We have managed the business side of Village Harvest conservatively. Through most of our thirteen years we have had one to three years' worth of cash expense in the bank; this enabled us to make decisions based on what's right for the organization without needing to find funds first. We have not been dependent on any specific grant and have been largely supported by our base of homeowners and volunteers."

So what are the biggest challenges of Village Harvest as it moves into the future? "Our challenges have not been financial to date," says Diserens. "Rather, our biggest challenges have been people related. What we do is operationally complex, we have a high standard for ourselves, yet we do it largely with volunteers. It has to be a satisfying and rewarding experience for them. Training and maintaining a high skill-level 'staff' of volunteer leaders is very challenging. We started with a fairly centralized organization approach, but over the years it would sometimes 'break' as key volunteers or part-time staff left or were unable to participate at the same level. After ten years, one of the founders was unable to continue, and in the same period our part-time harvesting coordinator resigned for full-time school. We needed to transition the leadership and make structural changes in the organization. Structurally we decentralized from one paid planner organizing all harvests into many volunteer planners organizing one or two harvests a month. This made Village Harvest much less dependent on a single individual, provided redundancy, and enabled growth into new communities. Going forward we now have the financial challenge of our budget growing fifteen times with the transition to regular paid staff and a fully funded director position. This is unsolved, although we're making progress at learning fund-raising, a new skill and need for us even though we're thirteen years old and very active."

Many founder-driven nonprofits, especially those as successful as Village Harvest, eventually get to the point where a succession plan is critical. Diserens is candid about the challenge of making this transition. "The 'keys' to our electronic infrastructure are now shared, we are documenting our systems and processes, and we have redundant people in key roles. But there are many things I do for the organization that would be difficult to replace quickly. In addition, the organization does not yet have the funding foundation in place to pay market rates for a replacement for me as the Executive Director."

Village Harvest represents an exceptional model of an organization that started small but soon grew to the extent that it recognized that it needed to evolve to successfully continue to serve its constituents. And Craig Diserens shares some valuable insights for emerging or ongoing nonprofits that want to focus on sustainability: "Focus on doing one narrow thing well with a clear social or community value to others, and do that exceptionally well. A clear purpose and outstanding results makes it easier to gain followers, gain financial support, and evolve. And while it's not directly about being sustainable, my other recommendation to nonprofits is to build great relationships with all kinds of constituencies. Much of our success comes from relationships, of sharing and helping each other. Nonprofits are a people business." And he adds a final, important coda for new projects and organizations: "Do not expect money first. Money comes later. *Passion, inspiration, relationships,* and *doing* come first."

Appendix II:
Access and Assets
Inventory Checklist

Your nonprofit's assets and inventory list may differ somewhat from this one, but you can easily build off this and adjust it to the particulars of yours. As a final note, it's common for a nonprofit organization to have multiple computers in different locations, so be sure to indicate which software programs reside in each of them.

To begin, copy and print this list. You may have other assets that you'd like to include. If so, scanning this list and using OCR (optical character recognition) software will enable you to electronically store the list on your computer.

Office Alarm

Company:
Phone:
Code/password:

Bank Account(s)

Name of bank:
Address:
Phone:
Checking acct. number:
Savings acct. number:
URL for online banking:
Username/password:
Name of signatory:
Tech support phone:

Appendix II

Credit/Debit Card(s)

Name of bank:
Card number:
PIN:
Expiration date:
Tech support phone:

"Donation" Button on Website, Linked to Bank

Name of provider:
URL for Log-on:
E-mail:
Password:

Organizational Memberships

Name of organization:
Address:
Membership number:
Username/password:
Website:

Telephone/Internet Access

Name of telephone company:
Account number:
Username/password/PIN:
Router manufacturer/model number:
Router serial number:
Router ID number:
Wireless Network Key:
How, when, to whom subscription is paid:
Tech support phone:

Computers and Hardware

COMPUTER

Make, model, serial number:
Location:
Username/password:
IP (Internet Protocol) address:
Tech support phone:

PRINTER

Make, model, serial number:
Location:
Tech support phone:

SCANNER

Make, model, serial number:
Location:
Tech support phone:

USB BACKUP DRIVE(S)

Make, model, serial number:
Location:
Tech support phone:

Software

WORD PROCESSOR

Manufacturer and version number:
File name and path:
Computer host:
Licensed to:
License or product ID number:
Number of licenses:
Tech support phone:

Appendix II

OCR (OPTICAL CHARACTER RECOGNITION) SOFTWARE

Manufacturer and version number:

File name and path:

Computer host:

Licensed to:

License or product ID number:

Number of licenses:

Tech support phone:

E-MAIL

E-mail platform/manufacturer/version number:

File name and path:

Number of licenses:

Computer host:

Username/password:

E-mail web host/URL:

Customer number:

Username/password/PIN:

How, when, to whom subscription is paid:

Server type, POP Mail Server:

Server name:

Port:

Username:

Outgoing Server (SMTP) name:

Port:

(If e-mail is on local hard drive) Mail server file location on local drive is:

Tech support phone:

E-mail web host:

How, when, to whom subscription is paid:

Tech support phone:

Access and Assets Inventory Checklist

CRM (CUSTOMER RELATIONSHIP MANAGEMENT)
Manufacturer and version number:
File name and path:
Computer host:
Database name:
Username/password:
Licensed to:
Serial number:
Customer ID number:
Number of licenses:
How and to whom subscription is paid (if any):
Tech support phone:

COLLECTIONS DATABASE
Manufacturer and version number:
File name and path:
Computer host:
Database name:
Username/password:
License or product ID number:
License number:
Number of licenses:
How and to whom subscription is paid (if any):
Tech support phone:

INTERNET SECURITY SOFTWARE
Manufacturer and version number:
File name and path:
Computer host:
Licensed to:
License or product ID number:
Number of licenses:
Username/password:
How, to whom, and when subscription is paid:
Tech support phone:

Appendix II

Financial Software

Manufacturer and version number:
File name and path:
Computer host:
Username/password:
Licensed to:
License or product ID number:
Number of licenses:
How and to whom subscription is paid (if any):
Tech support phone:

Photo-Processing Software

Manufacturer and version number:
File name and path:
Computer host:
Licensed to:
License or product ID number:
Number of licenses:
Tech support phone:

PDF Software

Manufacturer and version number:
File name and path:
Computer host:
Licensed to:
License or product ID number:
Number of licenses:
Tech support phone:

Backup Software

Manufacturer and version number:
File name and path:
Computer host:
Licensed to:
License or product ID number:
Number of licenses:
Location:
Tech support phone:

Web-Hosting and URL Data

WEB CREATION SOFTWARE
Manufacturer and version number of web software:
File name and path:
Computer host:
Licensed to:
License or product ID number:
Computer host:
Username/password:
How, when to renew license:
Tech support phone:

URL LICENSING COMPANY/URL
Manufacturer and version number:
Customer number:
Username/password/PIN:
How, when to renew license:
Tech support phone:

WEB-HOSTING COMPANY/URL
Manufacturer and version number:
Customer number:
Username/password/PIN:
How, when to renew license:
Tech support phone:

Other Internet Resources

TechSoup (http://www.techsoup.org/get-product-donations)
Username/password:

Collection Management

Name of collection space:
Address:
Phone:
URL:
Contact name/title(s) and phone numbers:

Repair and Maintenance

Provider name:
Contact information:
Service rendered:
Typical charges:

Potential Successor Organizations

Name of organization:
Address and phone:
Website:
Contact name and title:
Contact name phone and e-mail address:
What was discussed, including positives and negatives:
What would be potential next steps?

Chapter Notes

Preface

1. *Merriam-Webster's Collegiate Dictionary*, 10th ed. (Springfield, MA: Merriam-Webster, 1993).

Introduction

1. Source: IRS Business Master File 04/2009 (with modifications by the National Center for Charitable Statistics at the Urban Institute to exclude foreign and governmental organizations), http://nccsweb.urban.org/PubApps/profile1.php?state=US.
2. Mark Emmons and Jason Green, "Peninsula Symphony Struggles," *San Jose Mercury News*, October 12, 2013, pp. B1, B6.
3. Http://www.irs.gov/irm/part7/irm_07-025-003.html discusses religious, charitable, educational and other organizations under IRC 501(c)(3).
4. There are sixteen of them, as of this writing (http://www.irs.gov/publications/p557/ch04.htm)l.
5. Anthony Mancuso, *How to Form a Nonprofit Corporation*, 11th ed. (Berkeley: Nolo Press, 2013).

Chapter 2

1. Lyn Scott, *From Passion to Execution: How to Start and Grow an Effective Nonprofit Organization* (Boston: Course Technology, 3013), pp. 102–103.

Chapter 3

1. Author Peri H. Pakroo, J.D., offers several pages of pro and con arguments to incorporation in her book *Starting & Building a Nonprofit: A Practical Guide* (Berkeley: Nolo Press, 2013), pp. 13–22.
2. For full wording of RUUNAA as well as up-to-date status of adoption by various states, visit http://www.uniformlaws.org/Act.aspx?title=Unincorporated Nonprofit Association Act (2008).
3. For a lengthy but interesting analysis of UUNAA and RUUNAA, read Elizabeth S. Miller's "Doctoring the Law of Nonprofit Associations with a Band-Aid or a Body Cast: A Look at the 1996 and 2008 Uniform Unincorporated Nonprofit Association Acts," http://www.wmitchell.edu/lawreview/Volume38/documents/7.Miller.pdf.
4. Anthony Mancuso, *How to Form a Nonprofit Corporation*, 11th ed. (Berkeley: Nolo Press, 2013).
5. See Internal Revenue Manual (IRM) section 7.25.3.4: "Operational Test," February 23, 1999, http://www.irs.gov/irm/part7/irm_07-025-003.html#d0e673.
6. Http://www.irs.gov/Charities-&-Non-Profits/Charitable-Organizations/Publicly-Supported-Charities. See IRM section 7.26.3.2: "33⅓ Percent-of-Support Test," November 19, 1999, http://www.irs.gov/irm/part7/irm_07-026-003.html.
7. See IRM section 7.26.3.3.1: "Nature of a Publicly Supported Organization," November 19, 1999, http://www.irs.gov/irm/part7/irm_07-026-003.html#d0e303.
8. Http://www.sos.ca.gov/business/be/name-availability.htm#checking.

9. Audrey Wong, note to the author, May 16, 2014.

10. *Ibid.*

11. Jim Reed, note to the author, April 24, 2014.

12. Http://www.irs.gov/Businesses/ Small-Businesses-&-Self-Employed/ Online-EIN:-Frequently-Asked-Ques tions.

13. Audrey Wong, note to the author, May 14, 2014.

14. Mancuso, *How to Form a Non-profit Corporation*, 2013.

Chapter 4

1. David J. Neff and Randal C. Moss, *The Future of Nonprofits: Innovate and Thrive in the Digital Age* (Hoboken, NJ: John Wiley, 2011), pp. 61–62.

Chapter 5

1. David J. Neff and Randal C. Moss, *The Future of Nonprofits: Innovate and Thrive in the Digital Age* (Hoboken, NJ: John Wiley, 2011), p. 142.

2. In case you're looking, we at the AFA do not have a Facebook page. Instead, we focus all our efforts on evolving and maintaining our website of more than 150 pages.

Chapter 6

1. Alison Green and Jerry Hauser, *Managing to Change the World: The Nonprofit Manager's Guide to Getting Results* (San Francisco: Jossey-Bass, 2012), pp. 59–60.

2. *Ibid.*, pp. 172–173.

3. Peter Drucker, *Managing the Non-Profit Organization* (New York: Harper-Collins, 1990), p. 150.

4. Beth Kanter and Allison H. Fine, *The Networked Nonprofit: Connecting with Social Media to Drive Change* (San Francisco: Jossey-Bass, 2010).

5. Neil Blumenthal, "How to Manage Millennials," *Inc. Magazine*, November 2013, p. 48.

6. Lorenzo Milam's *Sex and Broad-casting: A Handbook on Starting a Radio Station for the Community* (Los Gatos, CA: Dildo Press, 1975), although published in 1975, is still considered to be the "go-to" book for starting a community radio station.

7. Peri H. Pakroo, J.D., *Starting & Building a Nonprofit: A Practical Guide* (Berkeley: Nolo Press, 2013), p. 88.

8. Audrey Wong, note to the author, May 14, 2014.

9. Green and Hauser, *Managing to Change the World*, p. 11.

10. *Ibid.*, p. 17.

11. Audrey Wong, note to the author, May 14, 2014.

12. Roger J. Davies and Osamu Ikeno, for example, discuss *Kenkyo*, the Japanese concept of modesty and humility, in the book they edited *The Japanese Mind: Understanding Contemporary Japanese Culture* (North Clarendon, VT: Tuttle, 2002), pp. 143–148.

Chapter 7

1. Steve Rothschild, *The Non Non-profit: For-Profit Thinking for Nonprofit Success* (San Francisco: Jossey-Bass, 2012), pp. 173–174.

Chapter 8

1. Rick Holden, conversation with the author, November 4, 2013.

2. Sandy Moll, e-mail to the author, November 5, 2013.

Chaper 10

1. Warren P. Everote, *My Odyssey: A Life in Educational Media 1946–1971* (2013).

2. Jan Everote, e-mail to the author, June 11, 2014.

3. Raymond F. Cavanagh, *The Amulet of Cananea* (2014).

4. Raymond F. Cavanagh, e-mail to the author, May 9, 2014.

5. Jonathan Kirsch, *Kirsch's Handbook of Publishing Law* (Venice, CA: Acrobat Books, 1996). Another worthwhile

book on a similar topic is Richard Curtis, *How to Be Your Own Literary Agent* (New York: Houghton Mifflin, 1996).

Chapter 11

1. Two of them were Laurie Blum's *Complete Guide to Getting a Grant: How to Turn Your Ideas into Dollars* (New York: Wiley, 1996) and Bev Browning's *Grant Writing for Dummies* (New York: Hungry Minds, 2001).

2. As Silicon Valley Creates' Grants Manager Audrey Wong notes, "It's typical of passionate, mission-driven organizations to go right to donors without doing homework—finding out what grantors want. Organizations with arcane missions have even more homework. But there are search engines out there. The Foundation Center has a directory and also holds free workshops" (https://fconline.foundationcenter.org).

3. These rebuffs were valuable in the sense that we knew we had to generate more publicity to underscore the importance of the films we were saving. That was a major impetus in writing the book that is described in the "Publicity and Publishing: Getting Others to Know About Your Work" chapter.

4. Snowden Becker, conversation with the author, October 14, 2013.

5. Snowden Becker, e-mail to the author, October 14, 2013.

6. Lyn Scott, *From Passion to Execution: How to Start and Grow an Effective Nonprofit Organization* (Boston: Course Technology, 2013), p. 102.

7. Andrew Bales, e-mail to the author, October 14, 2013.

8. Andrew Bales, conversation with the author, October 14, 2013.

9. Beth Kanter and Allison H. Fine, *The Networked Nonprofit: Connecting with Social Media to Drive Change* (San Francisco: Jossey-Bass, 2010), p. 114.

10. Such policies do change over time, so always read the fine print, regardless of the platform you use.

11. This point is underscored by Audrey Wong, who notes that crowdfunding only works if you already have a substantial online following.

12. Don Campau, e-mail to the author, October 29, 2013.

Chapter 12

1. Cygnus Applied Research 2012 Donor Survey, http://www.cygresearch.com/files/free/Exec_Summary-The_Cygnus_Donor_Survey_2012-US.pdf, p. 9.

2. Http://www.consumer.ftc.gov/articles/0074-giving-charity.

3. Http://georgewbush-whitehouse.archives.gov/cea/ERP_2009_Ch9.pdf.

4. Sid Kirchheimer, "Scam Alert: Say No to Pushy Magazine Sales," *Aarp Bulletin*, May 30, 2011, http://www.aarp.org/money/scams-fraud/info-05-2011/magazine-subscription-scam-alert.html.

5. Charity Navigator only evaluates large 501(c) (3) organizations that file IRS Form 990, with public support more than $500,000 and total revenue more $1,000,000 in the most recent fiscal year.

6. Audrey Wong, note to the author, May 14, 2014.

7. Stan Hutton and Frances Phillips, *Nonprofit Kit for Dummies*, 3rd ed. (Hoboken, NJ: Wiley, 2010), pp. 173–174.

8. Jane Arsenault, *Forging Nonprofit Alliances* (San Francisco: Jossey-Bass, 1998).

Chapter 13

1. KTAO wasn't a nonprofit but, as a noncommercial station, operated like one for much of its existence.

2. WorldCat (www.worldcat.org) shows that today four archives list the film *Cave People of the Philippines* in their inventory.

3. A similar protest occurred again in 1996, regarding a traveling show of Vietnamese and Viet-Kieu artists, titled *An Ocean Apart*. Same museum, same issues. Since that time, the San Jose

Museum of Art has staged one more artist-specific Vietnamese show (in 2003, by Vietnam-born artist Long Nguyen) and has included other Vietnamese artists in several group shows. For more on protest by San Jose's conservative Vietnamese element and their protests over artistic programs they consider communist propaganda, read author Stephen J. Tepper's book *Not Here, Not Now, Not That!: Protest Over Art and Culture in America* (Chicago: University of Chicago Press, 2011), pp. 203–204.

Chapter 14

1. "Old Battles and New Challenges" *Non-Profit Times*, April 1, 2002, http://www.thenonprofittimes.com/news-articles/old-battles-and-new-challenges/.

2. Teresa Carpenter, *Missing Beauty* (New York: W. W. Norton, 1988).

3. Scott Hensley, "Planned Parenthood Controversy Hangs Over Komen's Fundraising Races," June 1, 2012, http://www.npr.org/blogs/health/2012/06/01/154135526/planned-parenthood-controversy-hangs-over-komens-fundraising-races.

4. As History San José's Jim Reed relates: "In the early 1970's, at the request of a corporate office, a nonprofit botanical garden in the Midwest began providing 'plantscaping' services in an office building. Over time, the demand for such services increased, and the botan-

ical garden was generating fairly significant sales. A group of local florists brought suit, and the botanical garden had to cease that activity or lose its nonprofit status with the IRS" (e-mail to the author, May 14, 2014).

5. As always, consult latest IRS tax law for current regulations.

6. Peri H. Pakroo, J.D., *Starting & Building a Nonprofit: A Practical Guide* (Berkeley: Nolo Press, 2013), p. 247.

Chapter 15

1. For more on this possibility, read Jane Arsenault, *Forging Nonprofit Alliances* (San Francisco: Jossey-Bass, 1998).

Chapter 16

1. Ironically, more than fifteen years later the old Christian Science church in St. James Park remains vacant.

2. As Audrey Wong notes, "Oftentimes brick-and-mortar turns into a millstone that drags organizations under ... be careful what you wish for" (note to the author, May 14, 2014).

Appendix I

1. For more on how Plumas Arts has achieved this success rate, read chapter 11, "Grants, Consultants and Crowdfunding Platforms."

Bibliography

Books

Alexander, Geoff. *Academic Films for the Classroom: A History*. Jefferson, NC: McFarland, 2010.

Arsenault, Jane. *Forging Nonprofit Alliances*. San Francisco: Jossey-Bass, 1998.

Blum, Laurie. *The Complete Guide to Getting a Grant: How to Turn Your Ideas into Dollars*. New York: John Wiley, 1996.

Browning, Bev. *Grant Writing for Dummies*. New York: Hungry Minds, 2001.

Carpenter, Teresa. *Missing Beauty*. New York: W. W. Norton, 1988.

Curtis, Richard. *How to Be Your Own Literary Agent*. New York: Houghton Mifflin, 1996.

Davies, Roger J., and Osamu Ikeno, eds. *The Japanese Mind: Understanding Contemporary Japanese Culture*. North Clarendon, VT: Tuttle, 2002.

Drucker, Peter. *Managing the Non-Profit Organization*. New York: HarperCollins, 1990.

Green, Alison, and Jerry Hauser. *Managing to Change the World: The Nonprofit Manager's Guide to Getting Results*. San Francisco: Jossey-Bass, 2012.

Hutton, Stan, and Frances Phillips. *Nonprofit Kit for Dummies*, 3rd ed. Hoboken, NJ: Wiley, 2010.

Kanter, Beth, and Allison H. Fine. *The Networked Nonprofit: Connecting with Social Media to Drive Change*. San Francisco: Jossey-Bass, 2010.

Kirsch, Jonathan. *Kirsch's Handbook of Publishing Law*. Venice, CA: Acrobat, 1996.

Mancuso, Anthony. *How to Form a Nonprofit Corporation*, 11th ed. Berkeley: Nolo Press, 2013.

Merriam-Webster's Collegiate Dictionary, 10th ed. Springfield, MA: Merriam-Webster, 1993.

Milam, Lorenzo. *Sex and Broadcasting: A Handbook on Starting a Radio Station for the Community*. Los Gatos, CA: Dildo Press, 1975.

Neff, David J., and Randal C. Moss. *The Future of Nonprofits: Innovate and Thrive in the Digital Age*. Hoboken, NJ: John Wiley, 2011.

Pakroo, Peri H., J.D. *Starting & Building a Nonprofit: A Practical Guide*. Berkeley: Nolo Press, 2013.

Riddle, John, with Tere Drenth. *Managing a Nonprofit: How to Write Winning Grant Proposals, Work with a Board, and Build a Fundraising Program*. Avon, MA: Adams Media, 2002.

Rothschild, Steve. *The Non Nonprofit: For-Profit Thinking for Nonprofit Success*. San Francisco: Jossey-Bass, 2012.

Scott, Lyn. *From Passion to Execution: How to Start and Grow an Effective Nonprofit Organization*. Boston: Course Technology, 2013.

Bibliography

Tepper, Stephen J. *Not Here, Not Now, Not That!: Protest Over Art and Culture in America.* Chicago: University of Chicago Press, 2011.

Journal and Magazine Articles

Blumenthal, Neil. "How to Manage Millennials." *Inc. Magazine*, November 2013.

Kirchheimer, Sid. "Scam Alert: Say No to Pushy Magazine Sales." *AARP Bulletin*, May 30, 2011, http://www.aarp.org/money/scams-fraud/info-05-2011/magazine-subscription-scam-alert.html.

Miller, Elizabeth S. "Doctoring the Law of Nonprofit Associations with a Band-Aid or a Body Cast: A Look at the 1996 and 2008 Uniform Unincorporated Nonprofit Association Acts." *William Mitchell Law Review* 38 (2011–2012), www.wmitchell.edu/lawreview/Volume38/documents/7.Miller.pdf.

"Old Battles and New Challenges." *Nonprofit Times*, April 1, 2002, www.thenonprofittimes.com/news-articles/old-battles-and-new-challenges.

Online Articles, Blogs, and Newsletters

Barcus, Bob. "How Much Server Space and Bandwith Do You Really Need?" October 18, 2010. www.myapheus.com/how-much-server-space-and-bandwith-do-you-really-need.

Cohen, Rick. "Sarbanes-Oxley: Ten Years Later." *Nonprofit Quarterly*, December 30, 2012. http://nonprofitquarterly.org/governancevoice/21563-sarbanes-oxley-ten-years-later.html.

Fisher, Tim. "39 Online Backup Services Reviewed." April 2014. http://pcsupport.about.com/od/maintenance/tp/online_backup_services.htm.

Hensley, Scott. "Planned Parenthood Controversy Hangs Over Komen's Fundraising Races." June 1, 2012. www.npr.org/blogs/health/2012/06/01/154135526/planned-parenthood-controversy-hangs-over-komens-fundraising-races.

Peters, Chris. "Tips for Designing (or Redesigning) a Nonprofit Website." January 1, 2012. http://www.techsoup.org/support/articles-and-how-tos/tips-for-designing-or-redesigning-a-nonprofit-website.

Websites

Acronis backup software: www.acronis.com.

Blackbaud Nonprofit Social Media Primer: www.blackbaud.com/files/resources/downloads/WhitePaper_BBIS_SocialMediaStrategy.pdf.

Bloomerang: https://bloomerang.co.

Blurb: www.blurb.com.

BookBaby: www.bookbaby.com.

Booktango: www.booktango.com.

Charity Navigator: www.charitynavigator.org.

Connecting Up web analytics overview: www.connectingup.org/learn/articles/introduction-google-analytics.

CreateSpace: www.createspace.com.

Cygnus Applied Research 2012 Donor Survey: www.cygresearch.com/files/free/Exec_Summary-The_Cygnus_Donor_Survey_2012-US.pdf.

DonorPerfect: http://www.donorperfect.com.

Evite: www.evite.com.

Facebook: www.facebook.com.

Federal Trade Commission. "Before Giving to a Charity." www.consumer.ftc.gov/articles/0074-giving-charity.

Bibliography

Foundation Center: https://fconline.foundationcenter.org.

Friends of Hue Foundation: www.friendsofhue.org.

Google philanthropy page: https://www.google.com/giving/index.html.

Google Search Engine Optimization: https://support.google.com/webmasters/answer/35291?hl=en.

Google web analytics learning resources: https://support.google.com/analytics/answer/4553001?hl=en&ref_topic=3424286).

Hortisexuals: www.facebook.com/pages/Hortisexuals/263053410382452.

Hubspot: www.hubspot.com.

Intuit: www.intuit.com.

IRM (Internal Revenue Manual) section 7.25.3.4: "Operational Test." February 23, 1999. www.irs.gov/irm/part7/irm_07-025-003.html#d0e673.

IRM section 7.26.3.2: "33⅓ Percent-of-Support Test." November 19, 1999. www.irs.gov/irm/part7/irm_07-026-003.html.

IRM section 7.26.3.3.1: "Nature of a Publicly Supported Organization." November 19, 1999. www.irs.gov/irm/part7/irm_07-026-003.html#d0e303.

IRS Article 8, "IRC 501(c)(3) Tax Exemption Provisions," section 3: "Dedication and Distribution of Assets." www.irs.gov/publications/p557/ch03.html#en_US_2013_publink1000200064.

IRS Form 557 (Public Inspection and Penalties): www.irs.gov/pub/irs-pdf/p557.pdf.

IRS Public Charity Test: http://www.irs.gov/Charities-&-Non-Profits/Charitable-Organizations/Publicly-Supported-Charities.

IRS Publication 561, *Determining the Value of Donated Property*: www.irs.gov/pub/irs-pdf/p561.pdf.

IRS Publication 598, *Tax on Unrelated Business Income of Exempt Organizations*: www.irs.gov/pub/irs-pdf/p598.pdf.

IRS Publication 1771, *Charitable Contributions—Substantiation and Disclosure Requirements*: www.irs.gov/pub/irs-pdf/p1771.pdf.

IRS State Links (a collection of links to state government websites with useful information, including state sales tax data, for tax-exempt organizations): www.irs.gov/Charities-&-Non-Profits/State-Links.

LinkedIn: www.linkedin.com.

Lulu: www.lulu.com.

Moz.com Search Engine Optimization: http://moz.com/beginners-guide-to-seo.

Mozilla Thunderbird: www.mozilla.org/en-US/thunderbird.

National Association of Secretaries of State (NASS): www.nass.org/index.php?option=com_content&view=article&id=44&Itemid=471.

NetApp Volunteer Time Off (VTO) program: http://www.netapp.com/us/careers/life/giving-back.aspx.

Nonprofit Risk Management Center (state liability laws): www.nonprofitrisk.org/downloads/state-liability.pdf.

OurVolts: www.ourvolts.com.

PastPerfect Museum Software: http://museumsoftware.com.

PDFCreator: www.pdfforge.org/pdfcreator.

Plumas Arts: http://plumasarts.org.

RUUNAA unincorporated nonprofit association law: http://www.uniformlaws.org/Act.aspx?title=Unincorporated Nonprofit Association Act (2008).

Smashwords: www.smashwords.com.

Swiftpage ACT! Pro: www.act.com.

TechSoup: www.techsoup.org.

Toastmasters: www.toastmasters.org.

Trend Micro: www.trendmicro.com.

Bibliography

Unified Registration Statement (Fundraising Registration): www.multistatefiling.org.
United States Trademark and Patent Office trademark search system (TESS): http://tess2.uspto.gov/bin/gate.exe?f=tess&state=4803:29avj9.1.1.
Village Harvest: www.villageharvest.org.
Volunteer Lawyers for the Arts: http://www.vlany.org/legalservices/vladirectory.php.
Volunteer Protection Act of 1997: www.gpo.gov/fdsys/pkg/PLAW-105publ19/pdf/PLAW-105publ19.pdf.
WhoIs: www.whois.com.
WordPress: http://wordpress.org.
World Insects and Natural Wonders Museum: www.wowasis.com/travelblog/?p=981.
YourVolunteers: www.yourvolunteers.com.

Index

Index

Index

Index